Stefan Buczacki

Best
Winter Plants

Special Photography Andrew Lawson

HAMLYN

Publishing Director Laura Bamford
Design Manager Bryan Dunn
Designer TT Designs
Executive Editor Julian Brown
Assistant Editor Karen O'Grady
Production Josephine Allum
Picture Research Jenny Faithfull
Researcher Hilary Engel
Special Photography Andrew Lawson

First published in Great Britain in 1997
by Hamlyn
an imprint of Reed International Books Limited
Michelin House, 81 Fulham Road,
London SW3 6RB
and Auckland, Melbourne, Singapore and Toronto

Printed in Hong Kong

A catalogue record for this book is available from
the British Library

ISBN 0 600 59023 2

CONTENTS

Introduction 4

The Biology of Winter 6

Planning a Winter Garden 8

Cultivations in the Winter Garden 10

Shrubs 14

Trees – Non-Conifers 48

Trees – Conifers 52

Herbaceous Perennials 58

Ferns 70

Grasses 72

Bulbs 76

Bedding Plants 84

Alpines 86

Climbers 90

Index 94

INTRODUCTION

'I dreamed that, as I wandered by the way, Bare Winter suddenly was changed to Spring.' The poet in this instance was Shelley but it could equally have been any of half a dozen others, all of whom seem to have been obsessed with replacing winter with something else. They couldn't have been gardeners or, at least, not thinking gardeners, for the notion that winter is a dead and miserable season, the sooner done with the better, is a sad one indeed. Many a winter's day, I've walked around my own garden and felt that, if such a time didn't exist, I'd have to invent it. The covering of frost and rime can create works of art from the most moribund and pathetic of vegetation and, indeed, to some extent nature can make your winter garden for you, even if you contribute nothing

Clematis orientalis **'Bill MacKenzie'**

but neglect. But how much better the effect if you deliberately choose plants for their appeal in the cold months of the year.

There may not be as many plants in flower or as much colour overall in the winter garden as in the summer, but it is their relative scarcity that makes winter flowers so uplifting. Perish the notion, however, that this is simply a flower book, for the greatest joy comes from the combination of plant attributes that make up the winter garden picture.

Leaves of evergreen plants fall piecemeal during the year and so the overall effect remains constant, and the shape and shade of all-green leaves can be as appealing as variegations.

A few deciduous species don't drop their leaves until winter is beginning to overtake autumn; while a few, like beech, even retain their dead leaves most attractively right through the winter. Buds, on both evergreen and deciduous species can display attractive and unexpected colours, rich browns, reds or black, for instance.

Bark, especially when exposed on the bare stems of deciduous trees and shrubs can be strikingly effective, sometimes simply because the absence of foliage exposes its normal colour, sometimes, as in dogwoods and some willows, because the colour really does intensify.

Young shoots of plants that begin growth early like *Pieris* and *Photinia* can be strikingly colourful. Fruits, seeds and seedheads on woody and herbaceous plants of many kinds are left on with advantage for the appeal of their colour and shape, as well as providing food for winter birds. All these have their part

Pieris **'Flaming Silver'**

Elaeagnus pungens ‘Maculata’

to play and I hope that I can encourage you to select and plant more frequently with the cold months in mind.

If you have a large garden, there's no excuse for not including those plants, and there are several, that have a stunning winter part to play but then fade from view in the summer. The lovely though common variegated shrub *Elaeagnus pungens* ‘Maculata’ is a good example of this. Its vivid winter leaf colour fades dramatically with the onset of new growth in the spring. In a smaller garden, nonetheless, I concede that a plant must earn its keep for the summer months too and, for this reason, I've indicated the appeal that each of my chosen plants has for the remainder of the year.

As with almost everything in gardening, it's the vagaries of the natural seasons rather than the calculations of diarists that determine when particular plants are at their most appealing. In some years, an individual shrub may be in full bloom in mid-autumn while in another it will be approaching mid-winter before it gives of its best. Variations in locality will, of course, make for more predictable differences in the time of flowering or other appeal. I've tried to take a median course in my timings and gardeners in extreme southerly or northerly localities will understand that they will need to make local adjustments.

I've also indicated the approximate length of the time over which each plant has its greatest appeal (autumn to mid-winter, late winter, late winter to spring and so forth) and the length of these periods should be fairly consistent, even if the seasons themselves are pushed locally forwards or backwards.

THE BIOLOGY OF WINTER

Visitors to tropical countries frequently express the sentiment that it must be wonderful to have gardens full of colour and interest all year round. And people from Europe or other temperate regions who set up homes and gardens in the Tropics commonly take with them some of their favourite types of plant. So one is almost as likely to see roses growing in a garden at the Equator as in one in England. But what sad, drawn and spindly things they generally turn out to be. For what is so easily forgotten is that plants from temperate climates need a winter. They simply are incapable of flowering their hearts out and keeping their leaves for 12 months of the year. We wouldn't have the displays that we so admire in the summer if the resting period of winter hadn't come first.

As I hope will be evident from this book, I love winter in the garden and I love gardening for winter; but even if you don't fully share my sentiments, you will be bound to concede that the winter is a necessity if the summer garden is to thrive. So what is special about winter? What are the features to which temperate climate plants have adapted but tropical plants have not?

Sempervirum montanum

There are two: the fall in temperature and the shortening day length.

Almost all energy on earth originates with the sun and with the solar radiation that reaches us through space. The amount reaching any particular garden

Galanthus nivalis

Eranthis hyemalis

will vary locally with such factors as the density of the cloud cover, the geographical situation and, very importantly, the time of year, which dictates the angle at which the sun's rays strike. The two most important types of radiation for plants are visible light, which they need for photosynthesis and for the control of flower initiation, and the longer-wavelength, warming radiation tending towards the infra-red, which provides the temperatures required for growth.

All plants rely on rather similar basic processes in order to grow and, like all chemical reactions, these are either speeded up or slowed down by particular temperatures. For this reason, most plants grow best and quickest within the same overall temperature range: they grow little above 25°C (77°F) or below 5°C (41°F) and best between about 10°C (50°F) and 20°C (68°F). So tropical plants grow quicker than temperate species because the optimum temperatures for growth occur for a much greater proportion of the year. By the same token, all plants that occur in extremely hot or extremely cold conditions (cacti in deserts or alpines in polar regions), tend to be slow growing.

The total amount of radiation reaching the earth in our latitudes is much less in winter than in summer, so plants won't grow here satisfactorily all year round. Individual species may respond in a limited way by flowering in winter but there is not sufficient light and temperature for them to put on new shoot growth.

Local effects which tend to enhance or depress the amount of radiation present at any particular place are gen-

Saxifraga x apiculata

erally of more significance in relation to temperature than they are to light and day-length. An abnormally cold winter garden is more of a problem that an abnormally shaded one. This is because there's no critical cut-off point for visible light, below which growth fails. With infra-red radiation, however, there is such a cut-off; it's the point at which the amount of warming radiation becomes inadequate to prevent freezing. Any small factor which tends to tip the temperature downwards below freezing can be critical and while fully hardy plants in the depths of winter are usually well enough equipped to withstand this (which is in effect, a definition of hardiness), the occurrence of a late frost in spring after growth has commenced can be devastating, even to hardy species.

Most winter frosts arise when cold air is transported over the ground from one site to another and, the low-lying places where this dense cold air collects are called frost hollows. Most spring frosts, however, are radiation frosts: they arise when the heat loss from the soil during the night is greater than is compensated for by the day-time warming up.

And a clear sky in spring before the day-time sun provides very great warmth, can create just such conditions. The more important type of frost for plant life is the air frost: one where the temperature is 0°C (32°F) or less at a height of 1.2m (4ft); by contrast, a ground frost, which occurs when the temperature has fallen to 0°C (32°F) at or just above ground level, is of much less importance, for the basal parts of plants are usually less vulnerable.

PLANNING A WINTER GARDEN

Your approach to winter gardening should be influenced by the space that you have available. In a small garden, it's extremely hard if not impossible successfully to devote an entire area or bed to plants that have winter appeal but have very little for the remainder of the year. In these circumstances I would strongly advise you to disperse your winter plants around the garden so that no areas look noticeably uninteresting in the summer. And, of course, by doing this in a small garden, none of your winter plants will be very far from the house.

With more space, devoting an entire bed to winter plants makes a great deal of sense. In my own garden, I have just such a winter-colour bed as a counter to another nearby that is distinctly a summer planting, largely of old roses. But in a larger garden, your winter bed really should be close to the house. No matter how keen a gardener or lover of fresh air you are, you will inevitably be in the garden far less in winter than in summer and winter plants placed far from view will generally be winter plants lost. Put them where they can be seen and admired through your windows. There are, however, a couple of exceptions to this general maxim. The effect of some of the golden-foliaged evergreens (conifers especially) is lost when they're seen from too close at hand and they make fine focal points some distance from the house. The same is true for some of the dogwoods with brightly coloured first-year shoots that create a much more dramatic effect when seen from some metres away. Their colours appear far less distinct when they are growing just in front of you.

Taxus baccata 'Standishii'

Buxus sempervirens

I always feel that winter gardening is rather more about shape than colour. The colours of plants are there but reduced in number, range and intensity. Plant shapes are, however, very evident, whether simply seen through the crisp cold air of a frosty winter's day, looming mysteriously out of the mist or, best of all, thrown into dramatic relief by frost or a covering of snow. Some individual plants can be splendidly dramatic in winter however they are grown, but I find that formal gardens generally look better than informal ones in winter. Try a small formal area of clipped box or low yew hedge, with a few geometrically symmetrical beds and topiary clipped shrubs where they can be seen from your house.

Ligustrum ovalifolium **'Aureum'**

CULTIVATIONS IN THE WINTER GARDEN

We should always remember that, whether or not their visual appeal extends into the summer months, the plants that give us pleasure in the winter do remain in our gardens all year round. They need care and attention at all seasons, just like the plants of the summer beds and borders. They will require the same feeding, watering, pruning and attention to pests and diseases. Rather than give general advice for year-round cultivation, however, which I have covered in other books in the series, I shall concentrate here on those tasks that are peculiar to the winter.

Soil and Site

Winter is an excellent time to prepare a site for spring planting; it's a time for digging, given reasonably mild conditions. Although digging frozen soil does little harm, it can be extremely hard work and burying large frozen clods may result in them remaining as frozen 'pockets' when the surface soil has thawed.

When preparing a new planting site for perennials, always bear in mind that you will probably not have the opportunity to dig it again as thoroughly for several years. Whether it is an entire bed or a single planting position, therefore, it must be double dug. This entails

digging to two spades depth and incorporating manure or compost into the soil as the hole is refilled. With a single planting hole, this is reasonably straightforward. With an entire plot, however, you must work from side to side of the area, remove the soil to two spades depth and take this soil to the far end of the plot. In effect, this produces a trench about 40cm (16in) deep. Repeat this operation with a second trench, parallel to the first, using the soil from the second trench to refill the first, adding manure as you do so. So you work, a trench at a time across the plot until you reach the end when you use the soil from the first trench to fill the last.

Frosted conifers

The appeal of some winter plants depends on the persistence of their fruits

Planting

Although planting isn't generally thought of as a winter task, perennials may be planted during mild spells; and such periods do provide an excellent opportunity for moving bare-rooted plants which, of course, should only be disturbed during the dormant season. Having prepared the bed or individual position as I've described, fork in bone meal around the specific planting spot. Spread the plant's roots carefully in the planting hole and cut off any that are damaged. Gently replace the soil in the planting hole, moving the plant up and down to ensure that no air pockets remain. Firm the soil carefully as you refill the hole but don't ram it down hard. Finally, finish by making a small mound with the soil sloping away from the stem to prevent water from collecting at the base, freezing and causing damage.

CULTIVATIONS IN THE WINTER GARDEN

Feeding and watering

Although plants in containers may need watering in winter if their leaves form an 'umbrella' that keeps rain from the surface of the compost, plants in the open garden won't require this. They will nonetheless benefit in three important ways from mulching in the autumn. First it will keep the soil fairly uniformly moist during the winter; second, it will help suppress any weed growth once temperatures rise in the spring, and third, and very importantly, it will protect the crowns of the plants from penetrating frost. Ironically, a covering of snow plays a similar role in helping to prevent frost penetration and should never be cleared away from around the base of plants.

Feeding isn't a job for the winter; slow-release fertilizer such as bone meal may be applied in the autumn but I prefer to wait until growth is beginning in early spring.

Pruning

Although some plants are routinely pruned in winter (apple and pear trees among fruit and wisterias among ornamentals), dormant-season pruning is really a task for early spring. I would indeed generally discourage late autumn and winter pruning because the plant is left open to frost penetration through the pruning cuts. Leaving on dead shoots, moreover, will help to trap layers of slightly warmer air close to the plant and this will help to ward off the worst of freezing weather.

Prunus subhirtella **'Autumnalis Rosea'**

Propagation

Seed sowing, at least seed sowing outdoors, isn't a winter task. Those woody plants that are propagated by hardwood cuttings may, however, be multiplied in this way at any time between mid-autumn and early spring. Root cuttings, too, are always taken in winter when plants are dormant.

Crocus tommasinianus

Pest and Disease Control

Most pests and most diseases are, like their plant hosts, dormant during the winter. But that doesn't mean that we can and should do nothing about them. On the contrary, being in a dormant state means that pests especially are vulnerable.

Above all, the winter is a time for tidying and cleaning; paying attention to what I call garden hygiene. Look carefully for the residue of autumn pruning; piles of twigs and other woody material will harbour coral spot disease which readily transfers from dead to live plant matter and can cause serious problems on acers, wisterias and other ornamental plants. Look out therefore for the tell-tale masses of tiny pink blobs and dispose of affected material. And if you do see the symptoms on living plants, cut out all affected parts, cutting well into healthy tissue. It's perfectly safe to compost woody matter affected with coral spot if it is shredded first but otherwise is best bagged up for removal to the local tip.

General tidying away of pots, seed boxes and other equipment will help to eliminate hiding places of woodlice, slugs, snails and other pests that are troublesome when young shoots begin to emerge in spring.

There's only one chemical control that can be used during the winter but it is an important one. Eggs and, in some instances, adults of several pests, including many aphids, survive the winter on the bark of trees and shrubs and can be checked by means of a tar oil spray. This is used routinely only on fruit trees and bushes but will just as readily eliminate pests from ornamental deciduous plants too. Tar oil shouldn't, however, be used on evergreen plants as it will scorch the foliage.

Skimmia japonica (female)

SHRUBS

Aucuba Spotted Laurel

" I've been recommending aucubas for as long as I care to remember. And I can only repeat here what I've told countless fellow gardeners on many another occasion: they are the easiest and most attractive of all evergreen shrubs for winter appeal in practically every site in the garden, including the relatively limiting one of dry shade. "

WINTER APPEAL Evergreen, glossy leaves that may have variously patterned yellow-gold markings. Clusters of bright red berries on female plants, if grown together with male plants.
PERIOD OF WINTER INTEREST Throughout.
VALUE FOR REST OF THE YEAR Purple-green star-shaped flowers in spring and continuing attractive foliage.
SIZE 1.5 x 1.5m (5 x 5ft) after five years; 4 x 3.5m (13 x 11ft) after 15 years.

CULTIVATION NOTES
Very hardy, tolerating -20°C (-4°F) or below; best not in full sun and thrives in light to very deep shade; any soil, even very dry; no pruning necessary. Propagate by semi-ripe cuttings in summer or hardwood cuttings in winter.

Aucuba japonica 'Crotonifolia'

Recommended varieties
Aucuba japonica appears in many attractive varieties: 'Crotonifolia' is female, with yellow-mottled leaves; *longifolia*, a group of varieties with narrowly elongated, all-green leaves, most female; 'Picturata', male, darker green leaves with central golden blotches; 'Rozannie', bisexual, producing some fruits in the absence of a male plant, broad, barely toothed, all-green leaves; 'Salicifolia', female, very elegant with narrow willow-like green leaves; 'Variegata', female, the oldest form but still good with cream-spotted leaves.

Berberis Barberry

" There is no garden that wouldn't be enhanced by one of the 150 or more species and varieties of Berberis *now obtainable. Many gardeners think of them simply as spring-flowering shrubs, some with evergreen winter foliage appeal, but they can enhance the winter season at either end with the late autumn foliage colour of some deciduous forms and the early spring flowers of some evergreens. "*

WINTER APPEAL Some forms have glossy evergreen foliage, deciduous varieties have brilliant autumn colours, most have attractive red or black fruits.
PERIOD OF WINTER INTEREST Autumn to late winter.
VALUE FOR REST OF THE YEAR Purple foliage in some forms, yellow spring flowers.
SIZE Most of the popular varieties will reach about 1 x 1m (3 x 3ft) after five years, 3 x 3m (10 x 10ft) or more after 20 years; dwarf forms only about 60 x 60cm (24 x 24in).

CULTIVATION NOTES
Moderately hardy, most tolerating -10 to -15°C (14 to 5°F); most tolerate full sun, but pale-leaved forms better in light shade; tolerates most soils; pruning not essential but on mature plants cut out up to one-third of shoots each spring. Propagate by softwood cuttings in early summer or semi-ripe cuttings in autumn.

Berberis thunbergii atropurpurea

Recommended varieties

Deciduous: Berberis aggregata has mid-green foliage that turns red in autumn, pale yellow flowers followed by egg-shaped red fruits with a white bloom. *B.* x *carminea* 'Pirate King' has dark green leaves, yellow flowers, spherical red fruits. *B. dictyophylla* has mid-green leaves that turn red in autumn, yellow flowers and red berries with a white bloom. *B.* x *ottawensis* 'Silver Mile' has silver-and-purple variegated leaves, yellow flowers; 'Superba', deep purple-red leaves, small yellow flowers tinged with red, and egg-shaped red fruits.

B. thunbergii atropurpurea has purple-red leaves that turn bright red in autumn, pale yellow red-tinged flowers and red fruits; 'Bagatelle', a dwarf form with redder leaves; 'Dart's Red Lady', very dark purple leaves turning orange-red in autumn; 'Helmond Pillar', dark red-purple leaves and an upright habit; 'Red Chief', long purple-red leaves on red stems turning orange-red in autumn, purple winter stems.

Evergreen: *B.* x *bristolensis* has oval spiny leaves, glossy green above, greyish beneath, solitary pale yellow flowers. *B. buxifolia* 'Pygmaea' has leathery, dark green leaves and dwarf, tufted habit, rarely flowering. *B. calliantha* has shiny, prickly green leaves, large pale yellow flowers and black fruits with a white bloom. *B. darwinii* is a truly glorious plant with small, shiny dark green leaves, bright orange-yellow flowers and blue berries. *B.* x *stenophylla* has narrow, spiny dark green leaves with blue undersides, bright yellow flowers and blue-black fruit; 'Corallina Compacta' is a dwarf form with spiny stems, small leaves, and masses of bright orange flowers.

SHRUBS

Buxus Box

Box is the classic evergreen of the formal garden, and enjoying a resurgence in popularity with the renewed interest in this style of gardening. There is still something of a tendency, nonetheless, to think that its appeal is only really evident when it is clipped. While clipped box does look wonderful in the snow, it can also appeal on other levels: look at the wide range of leaf size and shape and the various forms with variegated foliage.

Buxus sempervirens

WINTER APPEAL Dense evergreen foliage, many variegated.
PERIOD OF WINTER INTEREST Throughout.
VALUE FOR REST OF THE YEAR Constant foliage colour; excellent for formal hedging or topiary.
SIZE *Buxus microphylla* will reach about 80cm x 1m (32in x 3ft) after five years and 3 x 4m (10 x 13ft) after 20 years; *B. sempervirens* about 1 x 1m (3 x 3ft) after five years and 5 x 5m (16 x 16ft) after 20 years, but some of its varieties may reach only a third of this size or less.

CULTIVATION NOTES
Very hardy, tolerating -20°C (-4°F) or below; thrives in sun or shade, variegated forms best in sun; tolerates most soils but best in a rich loam; pruning not essential but plants used for hedging or topiary should be clipped at midsummer and in mid-autumn. Propagate by semi-ripe cuttings in summer or hardwood cuttings in autumn.

Recommended varieties
B. microphylla 'Compacta' is very dwarf and compact with tiny, narrowly elongated and recurved dark green leaves. *B. sempervirens* has oblong, glossy, dark green leaves, with many popular and widely available forms including 'Argenteovariegata', with white-edged rounded leaves; 'Aureovariegata', gold-edged leaves with some gold blotches; 'Elegantissima', white-edged small leaves, irregularly shaped, very slow growing; 'Latifolia Macrophylla' rounded dark green leaves and a spreading habit; 'Suffruticosa', small leaved, slow growing but not dwarf although much the best variety for edging knot gardens or other formal beds.

Callicarpa

There are very, very few shrubs that have as stunningly lovely a display of winter fruits as the callicarpas. So why don't I see them in more gardens? Partly, without doubt, because not all are sufficiently hardy although there can be no excuse in the case of the Chinese Callicarpa bodinieri, *which should be in every garden in the land; even if in a few of them, it will benefit from a little shelter.*

WINTER APPEAL Brilliant foliage and fruit colours.
PERIOD OF WINTER INTEREST Autumn to early winter.
VALUE FOR REST OF THE YEAR Small pink flowers in midsummer.
SIZE About 2 x 2m (6½ x 6½ft) after five years, 4 x 4m (13 x 13ft) after 20 years.

CULTIVATION NOTES
The varieties that I recommend are moderately hardy, tolerating -10 to -15°C (14 to 5°F); prefers a sunny, sheltered site; any fertile, well-drained soil; prune previous year's growth back to young wood in late winter; propagate by softwood cuttings in summer.

Recommended varieties
C. bodinieri giraldii has pale green leaves, tinged with bronze when young, red and yellow in autumn, and masses of violet-purple berries; 'Profusion' is a more vigorous form with larger fruits.

Callicarpa bodinieri giraldii **'Profusion'**

Calluna vulgaris Heather

❝Because the true Calluna heathers are summer-flowering plants, I've considered them in detail in Book 10, Best Summer Flowering Shrubs and also in depth in Book 2, Best Foliage Plants. They gain admittance here because, as foliage plants, they have all-year round appeal (sometimes intensified in winter) and their dead flowerheads, if left, can be singularly pretty in the frost. ❞

WINTER APPEAL The evergreen foliage of many forms turns brilliant shades of red, orange or bronze.
PERIOD OF WINTER INTEREST Throughout.
VALUE FOR REST OF THE YEAR Green, yellow or gold foliage colours in spring and summer; masses of tiny pink, white or purple summer flowers.
SIZE The more vigorous forms will reach their maximum size of about 50cm x 1m (20in x 3ft) after five years; others only half this size. Most will become rather straggly in time and need to be replaced after eight or nine years.

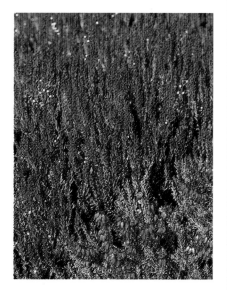

Calluna vulgaris **'Cuprea' (above)** with *Erica carnea* **'Startler'**

Recommended varieties
Among the most attractive in winter are: *C. v.* 'Blazeaway', yellow-bronze leaves in summer turning red-bronze in winter, purple flowers; 'Boskoop', orange-gold leaves turning red-gold, lilac flowers; 'Cuprea', gold leaves turning bronze, pale pink flowers; 'Gold Haze', gold leaves turning bronze, white flowers; 'Golden Carpet', yellow leaves turning red-bronze, pale mauve flowers; 'Golden Feather', golden leaves turning orange-red, pale mauve flowers; 'Mrs Pat', pink-tipped leaves turning dark red, mauve flowers; 'Multi-color', leaves turning from yellow, orange and bronze to deep red, purple flowers; 'Orange Queen', yellow leaves turning orange then bronze, mauve flowers; 'Robert Chapman', gold leaves turning orange to bronze then red, purple flowers; 'Sir John Charrington', a magnificent variety with yellow leaves turning orange with red tips, dark red flowers; 'Sunset', gold leaves turning orange, then bronze, mauve-pink flowers; 'Wickwar Flame', orange-yellow leaves turning bright red, mauve flowers.

SHRUBS

Camellia

❝ The 'Queen of the shrubbery' has regal appeal throughout the year and, in some varieties, those glorious flowers appear as winter draws to a close. But even when blooming is later, there's no denying the sumptuous form of the plants with their rich glossy foliage and plump buds. If camellias have a drawback, it is in their liability to shed the buds. ❞

WINTER APPEAL Rich, glossy foliage and exquisite flowers.
PERIOD OF WINTER INTEREST Late winter to early spring.
VALUE FOR REST OF THE YEAR Handsome evergreen foliage.
SIZE Most forms will reach about 1 x 1m (3 x 3ft) after five years, 3-4 x 2-3m (10-13 x 6½-10ft) after 20 years.

CULTIVATION NOTES
Fairly hardy, tolerating -5 to -10°C (23 to 14°F); best in a sheltered site with some shade; needs a peaty soil or acid compost; no pruning essential. Propagate from semi-ripe cuttings in autumn or leaf-bud cuttings in early spring.

Camellia **'Donation'**

Recommended varieties
'Adolphe Audusson', hardier than most, large, saucer-shaped, semi-double dark red flowers with yellow stamens; 'Akashigata' (syn. 'Lady Clare'), a big, spreading plant with large semi-double peach-pink flowers; 'Anticipation', paeony-shaped, deep rose-pink flowers; 'Berenice Boddy' rather tall and upright, semi-double pale pink flowers; 'Bow Bells', masses of cup-shaped, single rose-pink flowers with darker centres; 'Donation', profuse, cup-shaped, semi-double pink flowers, still the easiest and most reliable camellia for general planting; 'Gloire de Nantes', long-lasting, saucer-shaped, semi-double bright pink flowers; 'Inspiration', masses of saucer-shaped, semi-double pink flowers; 'Leonard Messel', large saucer-shaped semi-double rose-pink flowers; 'Saint Ewe', funnel-shaped, single, deep pink flowers.

Caryopteris

❝ It is alphabetical accident that brings together two of the best blue-flowered shrubs on the same pages. I have a slightly softer spot for the Oriental Caryopteris *than I do for the American* Ceanothus *but this may be because they are rather more demanding to grow and, in consequence, are seen less frequently. Very significantly in their favour, however, is their tolerance of highly alkaline soils. ❞*

WINTER APPEAL Brilliant blue autumn flowers.
PERIOD OF WINTER INTEREST Autumn to early winter.
VALUE FOR REST OF THE YEAR Aromatic grey-green foliage.
SIZE If cut back annually, will reach about 1 x 1m (3 x 3ft) by the end of the season.

Caryopteris x clandonensis

CULTIVATION NOTES

Moderately hardy, tolerating about -15°C (5°F); best in full sun and a light, well-drained soil; cut back hard in spring. Propagate by semi-ripe cuttings in summer.

Recommended varieties
C. x clandonensis has bright blue tubular flowers; 'Heavenly Blue', deeper blue flowers. *C. incana* has violet-blue flowers.

Ceanothus California Lilac

" Ceanothus are among the most successful shrub imports to European gardens from the west coast of North America. So much a part of our gardening scene are they that it's curious to realise that the important hybrid C. x delileanus wasn't produced until the 1830s and many species weren't introduced until even later. Their value as winter plants depends crucially on whether the evergreen or deciduous types are grown. And do remember that their blue shades are highly individual; they don't blend with everything. "

CULTIVATION NOTES

Fairly hardy, tolerating -5 to -10°C (23 to 14°F), but evergreen forms can be damaged by cold winds so should be grown against a warm wall; best in sun and well-drained soil; on deciduous forms cut the previous season's growth back in spring to 10cm (4in) from old wood; evergreen forms may have side-shoots trimmed after flowering. Propagate by semi-ripe cuttings in summer.

Recommended varieties
'T. Johnson', evergreen with long-lasting flowers in spring and autumn. 'Autumnal Blue', evergreen, long, loose inflorescences of flowers through summer and autumn; I think this is the best of all late flowering varieties. 'Burkwoodii', evergreen, bright blue flowers from midsummer to mid-autumn. *C. x delileanus* 'Gloire de Versailles', deciduous, pale blue fragrant flowers from midsummer to early autumn; 'Henri Desfossé', deciduous, large inflorescences of deep blue or purple-blue flowers in late summer; 'Topaze', deciduous, rich deep blue flowers from early summer to mid-autumn.

WINTER APPEAL Some forms bear their striking blue flowers in late autumn or occasionally early spring in mild years; some have lush dark green evergreen leaves.
PERIOD OF WINTER INTEREST Autumn to early winter.
VALUE FOR REST OF THE YEAR Some forms flower in early summer.
SIZE Deciduous varieties will reach about 1.5 x 1.5m (5 x 5ft) after five years, 2.5 x 2.5m (8 x 8ft) after 20 years; evergreen varieties about 2 x 2m (6½ x 6½ft) after five years, 4 x 4m (13 x 13ft) after 20 years.

Ceanothus **'Autumnal Blue'**

SHRUBS

Chimonanthus Winter Sweet

❝ There can't be a better advertisement for a winter-flowering shrub than to christen it the Winter sweet. Given good conditions, it will live up to this promise with exquisite fragrance, best appreciated when it's planted close to a house wall. But I stress that it must be given the best conditions. In poor soil, it has disappointed me; and bear in mind that the soil close to a wall isn't usually the best unless it's worked on with plenty of organic matter and fertilizer. ❞

WINTER APPEAL
Spicy, fragrant flowers appear on bare stems.
PERIOD OF WINTER INTEREST
Late winter to early spring.
VALUE FOR REST OF THE YEAR
Shiny, willow-like leaves.
SIZE 1.2 x 1m (4 x 3ft) after five years, 2.5 x 2.5m 8 x 8ft after 20 years. May not flower until at least five years old.

CULTIVATION NOTES
Moderately hardy, tolerating around -15°C (5°F), but in cold areas better against a warm wall; generally best in sun and a fertile, well-drained soil; no pruning if free-standing, but wall-trained plants should have all flowered shoots cut back in early spring to about 10cm (4in) from their base. Propagate species by seed in late spring, varieties by softwood cuttings in summer.

Recommended varieties
Chimonanthus praecox has very fragrant cup-shaped yellow flowers with purple centres; 'Grandiflorus', larger, deeper yellow flowers with red centres; 'Luteus', pure yellow flowers.

Chimonanthus praecox

Choisya Mexican Orange Blossom

❝ Choisya *has graced our winter gardens with its attractively divided leaves and rich glossy green colour since the early nineteenth century. Something like a century and half later, a yellow-leaved variant called 'Sundance' appeared to steal its thunder. I wish it hadn't. ❞*

WINTER APPEAL
Aromatic, glossy evergreen foliage.
PERIOD OF WINTER INTEREST
Throughout.
VALUE FOR REST OF THE YEAR
Fragrant star-shaped white flowers in spring and sometimes again in autumn.
SIZE *C. ternata* will reach 1 x 1.2m (4 x 4ft) after five years, 2-3 x 2-3m (6$\frac{1}{2}$ x 6$\frac{1}{2}$ft) after 20 years; 'Sundance' is about two-thirds of this size.

Choisya ternata

CULTIVATION NOTES
Moderately hardy, tolerating -10 to -15°C (14 to 5°F); thrives in full sun or shade, but needs shelter from cold winds, especially 'Sundance'; most soils unless very thin and chalky; pruning not essential but the oldest one-third of the shoots may be cut back to soil level each spring to promote new growth. Propagate by semi-ripe cuttings in late summer.

Recommended varieties

C. ternata is the most popular form, with mid-green trifoliate leaves; 'Sundance' has bright yellow leaves and fewer flowers.

Cornus Dogwood

❝ *The shrubby dogwoods provide some of the best twig and stem colour of all winter shrubs but please don't neglect their stunningly lovely winter-flowering relatives, the Cornelian cherries. Their spidery yellow flowers were the delight of many an English garden long before witch hazels were thought of.* ❞

Cornus 'Winter Beauty'

WINTER APPEAL
Brightly coloured young stems (most) or vivid yellow flowers on bare twigs (*Cornus mas* and relatives).

PERIOD OF WINTER INTEREST
Throughout.

VALUE FOR REST OF THE YEAR
Cream-white flowers in spring, some with variegated summer foliage, white fruits and/or colourful foliage in autumn.

SIZE *C. alba*, *C. sanguinea* and *C. stolonifera* varieties, if pruned every year, will reach a maximum of about 1.5 x 1m (5 x 3ft), otherwise about 2 x 2m (6½ x 6½ft) after five years and 3.5 x 3.5m (11 x 11ft) after 20 years; *C. mas* and *C. officinalis* will reach about 2 x 2m (6½ x 6½ft) after five years and 5 x 5m (16 x 16ft) after 20 years; *C. canadensis* will reach only about 20cm x 1m (8in x 3ft) after five years and 20cm x 3m (8in x 10ft) after 20 years.

CULTIVATION NOTES
All the recommended varieties are very hardy, tolerating -20°C (-4°F) or below; they need full sun or light shade, but will thrive in most soils, even heavy clay or light sand, except *C. canadensis*, which prefers a lighter, acidic soil; *C. alba*, *C. sanguinea* and *C. stolonifera* should have all shoots cut back to about 20cm (8in) above soil level in mid-spring; don't prune other species. Propagate *C. canadensis* by division in spring or autumn, other species by hardwood cuttings in winter or softwood cuttings in summer.

Recommended varieties

For coloured winter stems:
Cornus alba has red stems, dark green leaves turning red or orange in autumn, star-shaped cream-white flowers in spring followed by blue-tinged white fruits; among the best winter varieties, with similar flowers and fruits, are 'Elegantissima', red stems and grey-green leaves with white margins; 'Kesselringii', very dark purple-black stems, 'Sibirica' (sometimes called 'Westonbirt') and 'Sibirica Variegata', rich crimson-scarlet stems. *C. sanguinea* 'Midwinter Fire' and 'Winter Beauty' have wonderful yellow and red stems that look from a distance like a flickering bonfire. *C. stolonifera* 'Flaviramea' has bright yellow-green winter bark, oval, dark green leaves, white flowers and white fruits; 'Kelseyi' is a dwarf with very dense orange-red winter stems and brilliant autumn colour.

For winter flowers:
C. mas (Cornelian cherry) bears small yellow flowers on its bare stems in late winter and early spring, then bright red, edible fruits, and has dark green leaves that turn red-purple in autumn. *C. officinalis* is similar but lovelier with better flowers and pretty flaking bark, through more scarce;

For ground cover:
C. canadensis forms semi-evergreen ground cover with some red autumn colour, and green-purple flowers in summer surrounded by white petal-like bracts.

Corylopsis Winter Hazel

" Corylopsis are lesser-known relatives of that other 'false' hazel, the witch hazel, Hamamelis. They share its winter-flowering habit but their flowers are quite different in form, and are pendent, like the catkins of the real hazels. Winter-flowering shrubs are so much at a premium in our climate, however, that I can't understand why these beautiful plants aren't grown more widely "

WINTER APPEAL Fragrant, pendent inflorescences of pale yellow bell-shaped flowers on bare stems.
PERIOD OF WINTER INTEREST Late winter to early spring.
VALUE FOR REST OF THE YEAR Attractive hazel-like foliage in various shades of green.
SIZE 1.5 x 1.5m (5 x 5ft) after five years, 3.5 x 3.5m (11 x 11ft) after 20 years.

CULTIVATION NOTES
Moderately hardy, tolerating -10 to -15°C (14 to 5°F); best in semi-shade and fertile, moist, well-drained soil; pruning not essential. Propagate by softwood cuttings in summer.

Recommended varieties
C. pauciflora has bright green bristly leaves, bronze in spring with some autumn colour.

WINTER APPEAL Clusters of edible nuts; pale yellow catkins on bare branches in late winter to spring; *Corylus avellana* 'Contorta' has a particularly striking outline.
PERIOD OF WINTER INTEREST Autumn to early spring.
VALUE FOR REST OF THE YEAR Attractive bark, an unusual growth habit and/or ornamental foliage.
SIZE *C. avellana* and *C. maxima*, unpruned, will reach about 4 x 2m (13 x 6½ft) after 10 years and twice this after 20 years. Pruned annually, they will reach about 2.5 x 1.5 m (8 x 5ft). *C. a.* 'Contorta' is slower growing and will reach only about 5 x 5m (16 x 16ft). *C. colurna* will reach as much as 20 x 7m (65 x 23ft) eventually.

Corylus Hazel

" Few people have room in their gardens to grow sufficient hazels to produce a good nut crop, but many could still grow the various ornamental forms or even have one or two of the true species for the benefit of their catkins. They are utterly undemanding and are especially at home in the situation where many of them grow naturally: in mixed hedgerows of native plants. There is nonetheless a compromise to be reached because the varieties that are most productive of catkins don't have the most appealing foliage. Those that I recommend are the ones I have found achieve the compromise best. "

***Corylus avellana* 'Contorta'**

CULTIVATION NOTES
Very hardy, tolerating -20°C (-4°F) or below; thrives in almost any position, from full sun to deep shade, and in any soil; pruning not necessary in the varieties recommended here, but the ornamental gold- and purple-leaved forms will produce bigger, more colourful leaves if the oldest one-third of all shoots are cut back to soil level each spring. Propagate by layers or suckers.

Recommended varieties
C. avellana 'Aurea' has golden leaves; 'Contorta', striking twisted stems. *C. colurna* has attractive grey ridged bark and dark green leaves. *C. maxima* 'Purpurea' is a variety of filbert with rich purple leaves.

Cotoneaster

" *Cotoneasters are the essential all-season garden shrubs and the winter garden would be the poorer, from the point of view of both gardeners and birds, without them. Their appeal is often limited to the first part of the winter, however, by the birds themselves, for they find the fruits irresistible in a hard season, the deciduous forms can be bare by Christmas.* "

WINTER APPEAL Ornate evergreen foliage in some varieties; deciduous forms often take on autumn colours; almost all have brilliant fruits.
PERIOD OF WINTER INTEREST Evergreens throughout; deciduous forms autumn to early winter.
VALUE FOR REST OF THE YEAR White or pink flowers in summer.
SIZE Low to medium deciduous forms will reach about 60cm x 1m (24in x 3ft) after five years and 1.5 x 3m (5 x 10ft) after 20 years; low to medium evergreens include spreading types, such as *C. horizontalis*, which will reach about 50cm x 1.2m (20in x 4ft) after five years and 60cm x 3m (24in x 10ft) after 20 years, and others that may reach 1.5 x 3m (5 x 10ft) in the same time; tall deciduous forms will reach about 2 x 2m (6¹/₂ x 6¹/₂ft) after five years and 4 x 4m (13 x 13ft) after 20 years; tall evergreens will reach 3 x 3m (10 x 10ft) after five years and 5-7 x 5-7m (16-23 x 16-23ft) after 20 years.

CULTIVATION NOTES
Very hardy, tolerating -20°C (-4°F) or below; thrives in full sun or moderate shade and fairly tolerant of wind; succeeds in any but a very shallow chalky soil; pruning not essential. Propagate by semi-ripe cuttings in summer or hardwood cuttings in winter, and lower-growing forms extremely easily by layering.

Cotoneaster frigidus 'Cornubia'

Cotoneaster horizontalis

Recommended varieties
Deciduous: *Cotoneaster adpressus* is low growing with dull green leaves turning scarlet in autumn, white flowers tinged with pink, bright red fruits. *C. divaricatus* is tall with glossy dark green leaves that turn red in autumn, white flowers, deep red fruits. *C. horizontalis* is low with small rounded grey-green leaves turning deep red in autumn, tiny white flowers, red fruits.
Evergreen: *C. congestus* is low-growing with rounded dark blue-green leaves, white flowers, red fruits. *C. conspicuus* 'Decorus' is low with small grey-green leaves, masses of white spring flowers, red fruits. *C. x suecicus* 'Coral Beauty' is medium with small glossy dark green leaves, white flowers, orange-red fruits. *C. dammeri* is low with small dark green or red leaves, white flowers, dark red fruits. *C. franchetii* is tall and may be semi-evergreen, with grey-green leaves, white below, white flowers tinged with pink, masses of oblong orange-red fruits. *C. frigidus* 'Cornubia' is tall with long dark green leaves, masses of white flowers, bright red fruits. *C. lacteus* is tall with long dark green leaves, profuse white flowers, dark red fruits. *C. salicifolius* 'Pendulus' is medium-size with dark green leaves with purple veins, white flowers in early summer, red fruits; 'Rothschildianus' is tall with narrow bright green leaves, white flowers, golden-yellow fruits. *C. x watereri* 'John Waterer' is tall with dark green leaves, white flowers in early summer, masses of red fruits.

SHRUBS

Daboecia Irish Heath

❝ *I always consider* Daboecia *to be the 'forgotten' member of the heath and heather tribe. It's a two-species genus although only the hardier* D. cantabrica *is widely grown. It's a plant that, like the strawberry tree, has an odd natural distribution, along the western coasts of southern Europe and also on the western side of Ireland. I'd like it to be distributed in more peoples' gardens too.* ❞

WINTER APPEAL White, purple or pink flowers, evergreen foliage.
PERIOD OF WINTER INTEREST Early winter.
VALUE FOR REST OF THE YEAR Flowers start to appear in late spring and continue through summer and autumn.
SIZE About 20 x 60cm (8 x 24in) after five years, 20cm x 1m (8in x 3ft) after 10 years.

Daboecia cantabrica

CULTIVATION NOTES
D. cantabrica is very hardy, tolerating -20°C (-4°F), though the foliage may suffer frost damage; best in an open, position with an acid, humus-rich, free-draining soil; prune lightly after flowering. Propagate by softwood cuttings, division or layering in summer.

Recommended varieties
D. cantabrica has dark green leaves with silver undersides, and white, purple or pink bell-shaped flowers.

Daphne

❝ *Daphnes are small, rather aristocratic shrubs. They lack big showy flowers and large glossy leaves. But what they lack in dramatic effect, some more than make up for in their cold-season appeal. A penetrating fragrance from visually rather insignificant flowers often combined with evergreen foliage means that there should be room for one in almost every garden. They are also extremely easy to care for.* ❞

WINTER APPEAL Fragrant flowers and leathery, dark green, usually evergreen foliage in most of the varieties that I recommend.
PERIOD OF WINTER INTEREST Winter to early spring.
VALUE FOR REST OF THE YEAR Small, attractive black or red fruits follow the flowers.
SIZE Most forms will reach about 50 x 50cm (20 x 20in) after five years, and about 1 x 1m (3 x 3ft) after 20 years; *Daphne odora* may reach twice this height.

CULTIVATION NOTES
Most forms are very hardy, tolerating -20°C (-4°F), but *D. odora* is probably only hardy, tolerating -15°C (5°F); most forms are best in light shade and, apart from *D. mezereum*, generally intolerant of full sun; best in a deep, rich loam and tolerates some alkalinity; pruning not required and may encourage die-back. Propagate by semi-ripe cuttings in early or midsummer.

Daphne bholua

Recommended varieties

D. bholua has red-mauve flower buds, and flowers with white petals that have red-mauve undersides; 'Gurkha' is a hardier but generally deciduous variant; 'Jacqueline Postill' is also hardier than the species but evergreen and with larger flowers. *D. laureola* has yellow trumpet-shaped flowers followed by small black fruits. *D. mezereum* is a deciduous species with small pink or purple trumpet-shaped flowers followed by red fruits; *alba* has white or cream flowers ; 'Bowles' Variety' has larger, green-white flowers. *D. odora* has clusters of deep pink and white flowers sometimes followed by small red fruits; 'Aureomarginata', purple-pink trumpet-shaped flowers and gold-edged leaves.

Elaeagnus

" If there is one really reliable shrub with variegated foliage for all winter gardens, this is the genus to supply it. I have grown Eleagnus pungens *'Maculata' in every garden I have owned and would never be without it. But it has other relatives that are almost equally effective. They have the particular distinction of fading from view in summer when their colours are more dull. But in the cold clear air of winter, they truly shine. "*

WINTER APPEAL Variegated evergreen foliage in the varieties that I recommend.
PERIOD OF WINTER INTEREST Throughout.
VALUE FOR REST OF THE YEAR Constant foliage colour, scented flowers in late summer or autumn.
SIZE 1.2 x 1.2m (4 x 4ft) after five years, 3-3.5 x 3-4m (10-11 x 10-13ft) after 20 years.

CULTIVATION NOTES

All *Elaeagnus* are very hardy, tolerating around -20°C (-4°F) although they will suffer leaf browning from icy winds; tolerates shade, but best in full sun.

Thrives in almost any soil except very dry or very alkaline; pruning not required, but any plain green shoots on variegated forms should be removed. Propagate by semi-ripe cuttings in summer or hardwood cuttings in winter.

Recommended Varieties
E. x *ebbingei* 'Gilt Edge' has gold-edged leaves and small, highly scented bright yellow flowers; 'Limelight', gold blotches in leaf centres. *E. pungens* 'Frederici', narrow light green leaves splashed with cream; the most popular, 'Maculata' has dark leaves with gold patches.

Elaeagnus pungens **'Maculata'**

SHRUBS

Erica Heather, Heath

❝ *The value of heathers for the winter garden has, to some extent, taken a knock simply because too many people now grow them; or at least, grow them in a particular manner. The so-called heather or heather and conifer garden, a planting where they are grown to the exclusion of almost all other types of plant has, with some justification, been criticised. It's a hard, harsh type of gardening and even its strongest advocates now seem to concede that such displays are better when softened with bulbs, grasses and other perennials. I do hope that this will lead to heathers again being properly appreciated, for they are undeniably valuable for winter colour, both from foliage and flowers. And even dead heather flowers can be arrestingly lovely with the frost and dew lying on them. It's for this reason that I prefer to trim all heathers, including the summer-flowering types, in spring, rather than immediately after blooming.* ❞

Erica carnea 'Red Rover'

WINTER APPEAL Small, needle-like evergreen foliage which may be various shades of green, grey, silver or yellow, depending on variety; white, pink or red-purple flowers on winter-flowering varieties.
PERIOD OF WINTER INTEREST Throughout.
VALUE FOR REST OF THE YEAR White, pink or red-purple flowers on summer-flowering varieties; evergreen foliage may change colour in summer.
SIZE Most are rather slow-growing, ground-cover or clump-forming plants, reaching about 15 x 80cm (6 x 32in) when mature after about five years; the most vigorous forms, however, such as the summer-flow-ering *E. vagans* 'Mrs D. F. Maxwell', may reach 1 x 1m (3 x 3ft) or more. Generally, the larger the species will grow, the less hardy it is. Most tend to become straggly and untidy and, although this may not be a problem in extensive plantings, it can look unsightly in small gardens and the plants are there best replaced after seven or eight years.

CULTIVATION NOTES
Most are very hardy, tolerating -20°C (-4°F) although *E. erigena* is only fairly hardy, tolerating no less than -5°C (23°F); best in full sun but tolerates shade; summer-flowering forms must have moist, acid soils, but most winter-flowering types will tolerate alkalinity; trim lightly with shears after flowering or, better, in spring (see my comments above). Propagate by semi-ripe cuttings in late summer, or by layering.

Recommended varieties

Winter-flowering: *E. carnea* (Winter heath) varieties include: 'Adrienne Duncan', deep pink flowers, dark green, bronze-tinged foliage; 'Ann Sparkes', rose-pink flowers and golden foliage turning bronze in winter; 'Foxhollow', pale pink flowers and golden-yellow foliage; 'Loughrigg', dark purple-red flowers, pale green, almost bluish foliage; 'Myretoun Ruby', rich purple-red flowers, deep green foliage; 'Pink Spangles', pale pink flowers; 'Praecox Rubra', deep, rich pink flowers; 'Springwood White', large white flowers with brown anthers, easily the best white winter-flowering heather; 'Vivellii', deep rose-pink flowers and dark green foliage, a wonderful variety that I have grown for years; 'Westwood Yellow', pink flowers and yellow foliage. *E.* x *darleyensis* (*E. erigena* x *E. carnea*) varieties include: 'Arthur Johnson', deep purple-pink flowers; 'Darley Dale', mauve flowers; 'Furzey', rose-pink flowers; 'Ghost Hills', masses of pink flowers, and cream-tipped foliage in spring; 'Jack H. Brummage', pink flowers and golden foliage; 'White Perfection', white flowers and bright green foliage. *E. erigena* (Irish heath) varieties include: 'Golden Lady', low growing, white flowers and golden foliage; 'Irish Dusk', salmon-pink flowers and dark green foliage; 'W. T. Rackliff', profuse white flowers and dark green foliage.

Summer-flowering: *E. ciliaris* (Dorset heath) with pink or white flowers from midsummer to mid-autumn and grey-green or light green foliage. *E. cinerea* (Bell heather) has pink, purple or crimson bell-shaped flowers from midsummer to early autumn and dark green or purple-green foliage. *E. tetralix* (Cross-leaved heath) has white or pink flowers from early summer to early autumn and grey-green leaves that grow in a cross formation. *E. vagans* (Cornish heath) has white or pink flowers from midsummer to early autumn and light or dark green leaves with silver undersides. I have described these summer- flowering heathers in more detail and given my recommended varieties in Book 10 of this series, *Best Summer Flowering Shrubs*. But do remember that they must have acid soil.

Erica darleyensis **'White Perfection'**

Escallonia

66 *In areas mild enough for them to grow reliably, escallonias are excellent if not indispensable plants. They form lush green boundaries and good isolated specimens. In climatically marginal districts, however, where their evergreen foliage is likely to be browned in most winters, they can be a confounded and frustrating nuisance.* 99

WINTER APPEAL Rich glossy evergreen foliage.
PERIOD OF WINTER INTEREST Throughout.
VALUE FOR REST OF THE YEAR Inflorescences of pink or red flowers in spring and summer.
SIZE 2 x 2m (6½ x 6½ft) after five years, 3 x 4m (10 x 13ft) after 20 years.

CULTIVATION NOTES

Fairly hardy, tolerating -5 to -10°C (23 to 14°F); thrives in full sun or light to medium shade; any except the most alkaline soil; cut back one-third of the oldest flowering shoots to soil level after flowering unless grown as a hedge; propagate by softwood cuttings in midsummer.

Recommended varieties

There are many popular forms, differing little in winter appeal, all having glossy light to dark green leaves with grey undersides but with summer flowers in varying shades of pink and red,

Escallonia macrantha

Euonymus

66 *Euonymus japonicus has achieved some notoriety through my having persisted in calling it 'the public lavatory bush'. This is intended as a compliment and underlines its value as a screening plant, for which purpose it has been rather extensively planted around public lavatories. It is also, but for no connected reason, tolerant of salt spray and prone to mildew. In the winter garden, its rather hardier relative* E. fortunei *is of greater value overall for it has a number of most attractively variegated varieties.* 99

WINTER APPEAL Glossy evergreen foliage, variegated in many forms.
PERIOD OF WINTER INTEREST Throughout.
VALUE FOR REST OF THE YEAR Constant foliage interest; small summer flowers in some varieties.
SIZE *E. fortunei* will reach 60cm x 1m (24in x 3ft) after five years, and spread to about 3m (10ft) after 20 years; *E. japonicus* will reach 1.5 x 1.5m (5 x 5ft) after five years and 3.5 x 3.5m (11 x 11ft) after 20 years.

Euonymus europaeus

CULTIVATION NOTES

E. fortunei is very hardy, tolerating -20°C (-4°F) or below, though it may lose some leaves in very cold weather; green forms of *E. japonicus* are moderately hardy, tolerating -10 to -15°C (14 to 4°F), but variegated forms are barely hardy, tolerating 0 to -5°C (32 to 23°F); thrives in full sun to medium shade, although variegated forms are best in sun; any soil, even dry or sandy; pruning not usually required although upright growing shoots on ground-covering varieties of *E. fortunei* and also any reverted green shoots on variegated plants should be cut out. Propagate from softwood cuttings in summer or by layering.

Recommended varieties

E. fortunei is a prostrate, creeping or climbing plant with small oval glossy leaves; 'Emerald Gaiety', grey-green leaves with white margins that turn pink in cold weather; the frightfully named 'Emerald 'n' Gold', dark grey-green leaves with gold margins that turn pink-red in cold weather; 'Golden Prince', green leaves tinged with yellow; 'Kewensis', very small, mid-green leaves and slender stems; 'Silver Queen', cream-yellow leaves in spring, turning green with cream margins in summer; 'Sunspot', deep green leaves with yellow spots in the centre, an excellent variety. *E. japonicus* is upright and bushy with glossy dark green, toothed leaves and green-white flowers in early summer; 'Microphyllus Albovariegatus' has smaller leaves with white margins, and 'Ovatus Aureus' has larger leaves with yellow margins.

Forsythia

❝ *The yellow-flowered forsythia and winter-flowering jasmine are grouped together and sometimes confused in gardeners' minds as being among the easiest and most reliable of winter shrubs. To be honest, neither has a great deal of merit when out of flower, forsythia almost none. But the winter value of forsythia is so enormous that there should be room for a plant in all except the smallest of gardens.* ❞

WINTER APPEAL Brilliant yellow, bell-shaped flowers.
PERIOD OF WINTER INTEREST Early spring.
VALUE FOR REST OF THE YEAR Light to mid-green foliage may take on red-purple autumn colours.
SIZE 2.5 x 1.5m (8 x 5ft) after five years; 4 x 3.5m (13 x 11ft) after 20 years.

CULTIVATION NOTES

Very hardy, tolerating -20°C (-4°F); full sun to medium shade; any soil; remove the oldest one-third of the stems after flowering. Propagate by semi-ripe cuttings in summer, or hardwood cuttings in winter.

Recommended varieties

Forsythia 'Beatrix Farrand' has bright yellow flowers with purple throats, and autumn foliage colour. *F. giraldiana* bears pale yellow flowers especially early on purple-brown branches. *F.* x *intermedia* 'Lynwood' is one of the best varieties, with large, rich yellow flowers; 'Spectabilis', which I still think the best of all, may be even finer, with masses of long-lasting deep yellow flowers. *F. suspensa* (Climbing or Weeping forsythia) has narrow, pale yellow flowers on long, arching grey-green branches. *F. viridissima* 'Bronxensis' is a dwarf form with few lemon-yellow flowers.

Forsythia x *intermedia* 'Spectabilis'

Garrya Tassel Bush

❝ *Gardening friends will be rather surprised to find this plant in any book of mine. I don't think I have maligned any shrub more regularly over the years than this one, for the simple reason that I find grey catkins in grey weather to be singularly depressing. The very fact that my comments elicit such a strong response suggests, however, that a great many of my fellow gardeners view things rather differently; so here it is. Grow it if you must.* ❞

WINTER APPEAL Long, grey-green catkins on male plants, and glossy dark green foliage.
PERIOD OF WINTER INTEREST Late winter to spring.
VALUE FOR REST OF THE YEAR Constant foliage colour; clusters of small purple-brown fruits on female plants if grown near to a male.
SIZE 2.5 x 1.5m (8 x 5ft) after five years, 4.5 x 3.5m (15 x 11ft) after 20 years.

CULTIVATION NOTES
Moderately hardy, tolerating -10 to -15°C (14 to 5°F), but best grown against a wall in areas where the temperature consistently falls below -5°C (23°F); thrives in full sun to medium shade; best on a fertile soil, but tolerates most; no pruning required but may be cut back if necessary in late winter or early spring and winter damaged shoots removed. Propagate by semi-ripe cuttings in summer or hardwood cuttings in winter.

Recommended varieties
Garrya elliptica is the popular species; 'James Roof' is a male form with exceptionally long catkins although there is some doubt about just how true and consistent a variety it really is.

Garrya elliptica **'James Roof'**

Gaultheria

❝ *The genus* Gaultheria *in the family Ericaceae has now absorbed* Pernettya *and the hybrid x* Gaulnettya *to comprise a group of some 170 evergreen shrubs for gardens on acidic or at least neutral soils. Among the group are plants with enormous winter appeal because of their truly striking, colourful and relatively large fruits. Despite their vivid colours, the fruits are not among the first choice of birds, although this doesn't seem to be related to the fact that they are distinctly poisonous to humans. Nonetheless these are among the plants better avoided if you have young children in the family.* ❞

WINTER APPEAL Evergreen ground cover, foliage tinged with purple; rather large, spherical bright red, white, blue or purple fruits.
PERIOD OF WINTER INTEREST Autumn to early winter.
VALUE FOR REST OF THE YEAR Small, sometimes fragrant, flowers in late spring to early summer.
SIZE 50cm x 1m (20in x 3ft) after five years, 50cm x 3m (20in x 10ft) after 20 years.

CULTIVATION NOTES
Very hardy, tolerating -20°C (-4°F); best in medium to light shade but tolerates sun; needs acidic or at best, neutral, soil; pruning not required. Most easily propagated from suckers.

Recommended varieties

G. mucronata 'Bell's Seedling' has fruit of a rich crimson; 'Crimsonia', fruit deep red; 'Mulberry Wine', fruit deep maroon, darkening to almost black; 'Pink Pearl' fruit pearly pink; 'Wintertime', fruit pure white. *G. procumbens* (Checkerberry, Wintergreen) has red fruit, small white flowers and dark green foliage. *G. tasmanica* has vivid red fruit. *G. x wisleyensis* 'Wisley Pearl' has rich dark red fruit.

Gaultheria mucronata 'Signaal'

Hebe

❝ Hebes might seem an odd choice for the winter garden for the simple reason that most of them aren't hardy enough to survive the winter, let alone beautify it. The majority come from relatively mild parts of New Zealand but they do comprise a big group and among the 75 species are a few that will certainly enhance the cold months through their foliage appeal, although none are winter flowering. ❞

WINTER APPEAL Evergreen foliage in many shades of green, some glaucous; but strikingly different and cypress-like in the 'whipcord' varieties.

PERIOD OF WINTER INTEREST Throughout.

VALUE FOR REST OF THE YEAR Pink, white or purple-blue flowers from spring to autumn, depending on variety.

SIZE Low-growing forms will reach 30 x 80cm (12 x 32in) after five years, 50cm x 1m (20in x 3ft) after 20 years; tall-growing forms 1 x 1m (3 x 3ft) after five years, 1.2 x 3m (4 x 10ft) after 20 years; medium forms reach sizes between these two.

CULTIVATION NOTES

Most of the forms that I recommend are fairly hardy, tolerating -5 to -10°C (23 to 14°F), but the variegated types may be barely hardy, tolerating 0 to -5°C (32 to 23°F); best in full sun, sheltered from cold winds; any well-drained soil; pruning not required. Propagate by softwood or semi-ripe cuttings in summer.

Hebe ochracea 'James Stirling'

Recommended varieties

'Amy' is tall with purple-green foliage, deep purple flowers. *H. x andersonii* 'Variegata' is tall with grey-green silver-edged foliage, lavender flowers. *H. armstrongii* is medium-size with olive-green whipcord foliage, sometimes small white flowers. 'Autumn Glory' is low with purple-green foliage, deep purple-blue flowers. *H. cupressoides* is medium-size with grey-green conifer-like whipcord foliage, small pale blue flowers; 'Boughton Dome', a dwarf form with silver-green foliage. *H. x franciscana* 'Variegata' has elongated leaves with yellow margins and spotting, especially evident in winter, flowers purple but sparse in my experience. 'Great Orme' is tall with light green foliage, large pink flowers. 'Loganioides' is small with bright green whipcord foliage, flowers white with pink veining. *H. ochracea* 'James Stirling' is medium-size with green-gold whipcord foliage, sometimes small white flowers; probably the best of the whipcord varieties. *H. pinguifolia* 'Pagei' is low-growing with glaucous grey-green foliage, masses of small white flowers. *H. rakaiensis* is tall, forming a most attractive dome-shaped mound, bright green foliage, masses of white flowers sometimes marked with blue. *H. salicifolia* is tall with light green lanceolate foliage, masses of white flowers.

SHRUBS

Jasminum Jasmine

I recently asked some colleagues which plant they would recommend if they had to guarantee flowers in the garden on Christmas Day. By a large majority, the winter-flowering jasmine was the most popular choice. A few tiny sprigs, taken indoors to bloom, brings pleasure to the darkest winter day.

WINTER APPEAL *Jasminum nudiflorum* has small bright yellow flowers on dark green stems.
PERIOD OF WINTER INTEREST Throughout.
VALUE FOR REST OF THE YEAR Small dark green leaves, arching stems.
SIZE 1.5 x 1.5m (5 x 5ft) after five years, 3 x 3m (10 x 10ft) after 20 years.

CULTIVATION NOTES
Very hardy, tolerating -20°C (-4°F); thrives in full sun or medium shade; any soil, even very poor; cut back the oldest one-third of the flowering shoots in spring to promote new growth. Propagate from semi-ripe cuttings in early summer.

Recommended varieties
The normal species, J. nudiflorum is quite definitely the one to grow; there is a yellow-leaved variant, 'Aureum' but the rather sickly yellow of the foliage detracts from the flowers and it tends, in any event, to revert to green.

Jasminum nudiflorum

Laurus Sweet Bay

I often remind gardeners that while spices are tropical and tend to come from shrubs and trees, herbs are temperate and most likely to be herbaceous. The sweet bay, which in mild areas can attain tree size, is an exception to the rule although it is generally grown as an ornamental rather than a herbal plant. It is an essential shrub for the formal garden in winter or summer and although those rather distinctive, neatly clipped specimens tend to divide gardeners' opinions, few would deny that they look remarkably attractive in the snow.

WINTER APPEAL Aromatic glossy evergreen foliage.
PERIOD OF WINTER INTEREST Throughout.
VALUE FOR REST OF THE YEAR Small yellow-green flowers in spring; purple-black berries on female plants in autumn.
SIZE 1.5 x 1m (5 x 3ft) after five years, 5 x 4m (16 x 13ft) after 20 years.

CULTIVATION NOTES
Moderately hardy, tolerating -10 to -15°C (14 to 5°F), but the leaves are commonly scorched by cold winds; best in full sun to medium shade but tolerates deep shade; prefers a light open soil but tolerates almost any; pruning not essential but may be clipped to shape or cut back very hard if required (and this may be necessary after very cold winters). Propagate by semi-ripe cuttings in midsummer.

Laurus nobilis

Recommended varieties
Laurus nobilis is the most popular form, with dark green elliptic leaves that have grey undersides.

Ligustrum Privet

" *Much maligned these days as a hedging plant, there's no denying that privet is easy to grow. And although the normal green hedge species may be monotonous, a specimen of the golden form will brighten up any winter garden; although it is less hardy, but do be aware that in very severe weather, all types are prone to lose their leaves.* "

WINTER APPEAL Evergreen foliage, sometimes variegated, in various colours and shapes.
PERIOD OF WINTER INTEREST Throughout.
VALUE FOR REST OF THE YEAR Mustily scented flowers in summer.
SIZE Most will reach 2-3 x 2-3m (6½-10 x 6½-10ft) after five years and 6-8 x 6-8m (20-25 x 20-25ft) after 20 years, but *L. japonicum* 'Rotundifolium' will reach only 50 x 30cm (20 x 12in) after five years and 1 x 1m (3 x 3ft) after 20 years.

CULTIVATION NOTES
L. ovalifolium is very hardy, tolerating -20°C (-4°F) or below; other forms are moderately hardy, tolerating -15°C (5°F); *L. japonicum* Rotundifolium' is best in light shade, but other forms thrive in full sun to medium shade; almost any soil unless extremely wet or dry, or very alkaline; clip in spring if required. Propagate by semi-ripe cuttings in midsummer or hardwood cuttings in winter.

Recommended varieties
L. japonicum 'Rotundifolium' has rounded, leathery dark green glossy leaves with grey-green dull undersides, and sometimes white flowers in midsummer. *L. lucidum* 'Excelsum Superbum' has deep yellow- or cream-edged and mottled leaves, and large inflorescences of flowers in late summer. *L. ovalifolium* is the familiar hedging privet with oval, mid- to dark green glossy leaves with paler undersides, and short inflorescences of flowers in midsummer; its lovely golden form, 'Aureum' (Golden privet) has golden leaves, generally with slightly more green centres.

Ligustrum ovalifolium 'Aureum'

SHRUBS

Lonicera Honeysuckle

    Honeysuckles are climbers. They endow the garden with a heavy sweet fragrance that is simply redolent of balmy summer evenings; and so it has been for centuries. Thus goes conventional gardening wisdom. And yet I am here offering to you a honeysuckle that doesn't climb, doesn't flower in summer and has only been in European gardens since 1845. So be introduced to one of the most under-appreciated members of its genus, the Chinese shrubby winter honeysuckle.

WINTER APPEAL Small, fragrant flowers borne in mild weather; evergreen in warmer winters, but deciduous in cold ones.
PERIOD OF WINTER INTEREST Late autumn to mid-spring.
VALUE FOR REST OF THE YEAR Sometimes red fruits in spring; some autumn foliage colour.
SIZE 1.2 x 2m (4 x 6½ft) after five years, 2.5 x 3m (8 x 10ft) after 20 years.

Lonicera x purpusii

Recommended varieties
Lonicera fragrantissima has cream-white flowers and dark green leaves tinged with purple that are paler underneath.

CULTIVATION NOTES
Very hardy, tolerating -20°C (-4°F) or below; prefers light to medium shade, but tolerates full sun; may be grown against a wall or in open ground; any soil, even if relatively dry; pruning not required. Propagate from semi-ripe cuttings in early summer.

Mahonia

    The biblical quotation, 'Faith, hope, charity, these three; but the greatest of these is charity' could equally apply to the genus Mahonia, *among which 'Charity' is the finest variety of* Mahonia x media, *with 'Faith' and 'Hope' as two also-rans. But even though 'Charity' may be the best, it's the best among a distinguished company of plants for late winter and early spring. All are yellow flowered, all are more or less fragrant and all are relatively easy, though a few of them are a touch tender.*

WINTER APPEAL Inflorescences of yellow, usually fragrant flowers among striking evergreen foliage, followed by blue-black fruits.
PERIOD OF WINTER INTEREST Late autumn to spring, depending on variety.
VALUE FOR REST OF THE YEAR Useful ground-cover or statuesque specimen plants; foliage may change colour through the seasons.
SIZE *M. aquifolium* as a specimen shrub or, in massed planting, a rather tall ground-cover plant, reaches 80cm x 1m (32in x 3ft) after five years and 1 x 3m (3 x 10ft) after 20 years; most other forms will reach about 1.5 x 2m (5 x 6½ft) after five years and 3.5 x 3m (11 x 10ft) after 20 years, though the *M. x media* varieties may grow to 5m (16ft) or more.

CULTIVATION NOTES
Most forms are very hardy, tolerating -20°C (-4°F) or below, though foliage may be scorched by very cold winds, but *M. lomariifolia* is barely hardy, tolerating 0 to -5°C (32 to 23°F); *M. aquifolium* thrives in full sun to deep shade, *M. x media* in full sun to light shade, other forms are best in light shade; thrives in most soils but intolerant of extreme dryness; *M. japonica* and *M. x media* when young should have the terminal clusters of foliage removed after flowering to encourage branching, then, when mature, flowering shoots cut back annually after flowering and fruiting; other forms when mature should have the oldest one-third of the flowering

shoots cut back to soil level to promote new growth. Difficult to propagate by cuttings though semi-ripe cuttings in early summer may succeed; alternatively by layering or removal of suckers when present.

Mahonia x media 'Charity'

Recommended varieties

M. aquifolium 'Apollo' is vigorous, with upright inflorescences of bright yellow flowers in early spring and bright red-green foliage that turns purple-green in winter. *M. japonica* has inflorescences of upright, then weeping, very fragrant lemon-yellow flowers in winter and spiny, diamond-shaped leaflets that are dark green on acid soil, red-green on alkaline; 'Bealei' has shorter, more erect flowers and red-green leaves. *M. lomariifolia* has upright inflorescences of fragrant deep yellow flowers in late autumn to mid-winter, and dark to olive-green pinnate leaves. *M. x media* has several good varieties including 'Buckland', with dense inflorescences; 'Charity', whose flowers are upright at first then weeping; 'Lionel Fortescue', very vigorous, with thick clusters of fragrant flowers in upright inflorescences; 'Winter Sun', bright yellow flowers and dark green foliage. *M. x wagneri* 'Undulata' has short upright inflorescences borne in clusters at leaf axils in late winter and early spring, and spiky olive-green red-tinged leaves, silvery underneath, that turn purple-red in autumn.

WINTER APPEAL Attractive gold-brown catkins on bare branches.
PERIOD OF WINTER INTEREST Early spring.
VALUE FOR REST OF THE YEAR Attractive, aromatic foliage; clusters of yellow-brown fruits.
SIZE *Myrica gale* will reach its full size of around 1-1.5 x 1m (3-5 x 3ft) after about eight years.

CULTIVATION NOTES

Fairly hardy, tolerating -5 to -10°C (23 to 14°F); best in full sun or very light shade; needs a very damp, acid soil; pruning not advisable. Propagate by semi-ripe cuttings in early spring, by seed or, easiest, by removal of suckers.

Myrica gale

Myrica Bog Myrtle

❝ *Bog-garden shrubs are rather few at the best of times. Bog garden shrubs that have appeal in winter can be counted on very few fingers indeed. The bog myrtle is one of them although, in truth, any garden with wet, acidic soil and mild conditions can grow it. Any garden lacking these conditions will have to manage without.* ❞

Recommended varieties

M. gale (Sweet gale, Bog myrtle) is a deciduous species bearing shiny golden-brown catkins in early spring on both male and female plants, and has dark green or green-red aromatic leaves.

Osmanthus

" Osmanthus aren't especially hardy and so are rather unfamiliar to gardeners from colder areas. And it's for this reason that when seen for the first time, they tend to be dismissed as 'just another holly'. But holly they are not; and are quite unrelated, belonging instead and perhaps improbably, to the Olive family. It's in winter that the difference from holly becomes most apparent for, instead of red or yellow fruits, the plants are adorned with the most delightfully fragrant flowers. It's then that I wish my own garden was more mild. "

Osmanthus heterophyllus **'Variegatus'**

WINTER APPEAL Fragrant white flowers, holly-like evergreen foliage.
PERIOD OF WINTER INTEREST Autumn to spring, depending on variety.
VALUE FOR REST OF THE YEAR Constant foliage interest.
SIZE 2 x 2m (6½ x 6½ft) after five years, 4 x 4m (13 x 13ft) after 20 years.

CULTIVATION NOTES

Most forms are fairly hardy, tolerating -5 to -10°C (23 to 14°F); best in light, dappled shade but tolerates full sun thrives in most soils if well-drained; pruning not required. Propagate by semi-ripe cuttings in early summer.

Recommended varieties
Osmanthus armatus has cream-white flowers in autumn followed by dark purple fruit, thick, dark green, lanceolate, toothed leaves. *O. x burkwoodii* has clusters of very sweetly-scented flowers in early to mid-spring, leathery, ovate, toothed leaves with silvery undersides. *O. fragrans* has very fragrant tubular flowers in autumn, sometimes in spring and summer also, followed by blue-black fruits, leathery, oblong, toothed leaves. *O. heterophyllus* 'Aureomarginatus' has flowers in late summer or autumn, blue-black fruit and yellow-edged holly-like leaves. *O. yunnanensis* has cream-white flowers in late winter to early spring, followed by purple fruit, oblong glossy dark green leaves with black spots beneath.

Photinia

" There are plants whose winter appeal lies in their flowers, there are also those with attractive fruits or coloured bark but rather few in which the appeal is in the vivid colour of the unfolding shoots as winter eases its way into spring. The alphabet juxtaposes two of them, quite unrelated but sometimes confused. If this type of shrub appeals to you, however, be aware of one very important difference between Photinia *and* Pieris: Photinia *is lime tolerant, whereas* Pieris *isn't.* "

WINTER APPEAL Brilliant young shoots in evergreen varieties, autumn colour in others.
PERIOD OF WINTER INTEREST Throughout.
VALUE FOR REST OF THE YEAR Constant foliage interest in evergreen varieties; flowers and fruit in others.
SIZE 1.5 x 2m (5 x 6 1/2ft) after five years, 4 x 4m (13 x 13ft) after 20 years.

CULTIVATION NOTES

Moderately hardy, tolerating -10 to -15°C (14 to 5°F), though young foliage may be damaged by extreme cold; thrives in full sun to light shade, with some shelter from wind; generally best on acid to neutral soils but tolerant of some alkalinity; pruning not required. Propagate by semi-ripe cuttings in early summer.

Recommended varieties

P. davidiana is semi-evergreen with lanceolate, leathery dark green leaves, older ones turning red in autumn, inflorescences of small white flowers in midsummer followed by bright red berries; 'Palette', slower-growing with cream-edged leaves; *undulata* 'Fructo Luteo', yellow fruit. *P. x fraseri* 'Red Robin', much the best known and popular variety, is evergreen with dazzling red young foliage shoots from autumn through winter that turn bronze in late spring and summer. *P. glabra* has dark evergreen leaves that are red when young, and inflorescences of small white flowers in midsummer followed by red fruits that later turn black. 'Redstart' has dark evergreen leaves that are coppery-red when young, inflorescences of small white flowers in early summer followed by orange-red fruits.

Photinia x fraseri **'Red Robin'**

Pieris

" In drawing attention to the resemblance between Photinia *and* Pieris, *I have omitted one important feature of* Pieris *and one that does underline the importance of planning your garden for year-round appeal. While the attractive young shoots are an undoubted feature,* Pieris *is well worth growing for its flowers alone. "*

WINTER APPEAL Spectacular colours of new shoots on glossy evergreen foliage.
PERIOD OF WINTER INTEREST Attractive foliage throughout the winter; young shoots appear in spring.
VALUE FOR REST OF THE YEAR Masses of exquisite flowers in spring; constant foliage interest.
SIZE 80cm x 1m (32in x 3ft) after five years, 2 x 4m (6½ x 13ft) after 20 years.

Recommended varieties

P. floribunda, one of the hardiest, has red young foliage with erect inflorescences of white flowers. 'Forest Flame' has brilliant red young foliage that turns pink, cream-white and eventually green, white inflorescences. *P. japonica* has copper-red young foliage and waxy white flowers; among its most attractive varieties are: 'Blush', pale pink flowers opening from dark pink buds; 'Debutante', low-growing with masses of white flowers; 'Firecrest',

Pieris **'Flaming Silver'**

CULTIVATION NOTES
Fairly hardy, tolerating -5 to -10°C (23 to 14°F), though young foliage may be damaged by frost; best in light shade, with shelter from cold winds; needs a moist, rich, acid soil; pruning not required. Propagate by semi-ripe cuttings in early summer, or layers.

bright red young foliage and scented white flowers; 'Grayswood', brown-red new foliage; 'Little Heath', dwarf with pink-flushed young foliage edged with silver-white; 'Little Heath Green' is a non-variegated version; 'Mountain Fire', red young foliage that turns chestnut-brown; 'Pink Delight',bronze young foliage and white flowers opening from pink buds; 'Purity', compact with pale green young foliage and pure white flowers; 'Valley Valentine', masses of dark red flowers.

SHRUBS

Prunus

❝ Prunus *is a huge genus that embraces plants grown for a wide variety of reasons. There are several tree-sized species with winter appeal (page 51) but two smaller ones also, usually clipped to shrub size. The cherry laurel,* P. laurocerasus, *is one of the oldest of hedging plants but still valuable; the smaller-leaved* P. lusitanica *makes a good clipped specimen.* ❞

WINTER APPEAL Attractive evergreen foliage.
PERIOD OF WINTER INTEREST Throughout.
VALUE FOR REST OF THE YEAR Small white flowers, sometimes fragrant, in spring.
SIZE *P. laurocerasus* will reach about 3 x 3m (10 x 10ft) after five years and 8 x 8m (25 x 25ft) after 20 years, *P. lusitanica* about 1 x 1m (3 x 3ft) after five years and 5 x 5m (16 x 16ft) after 20 years. Both, however, are usually pruned or clipped to limit this ambition.

Prunus laurocerasus

Recommended varieties
P. laurocerasus has glossy bright green leaves that darken with age, and, on mature wood, inflorescences of fragrant, small white flowers in mid-spring followed by bright red fruits that later turn black; 'Otto Luyken', a compact form with narrow leaves, often flowers again in autumn. *P. lusitanica* has glossy dark green leaves with red veins and red stalks, and, on mature wood, scented flowers in early summer; *azorica*, lower-growing with larger, slightly curled bright green leaves tinted with red.

CULTIVATION NOTES
Very hardy, tolerating -20°C (-4°F) or below; *P. laurocerasus* thrives in full sun to heavy shade, but *P. lusitanica* is best in light to medium shade; most soils, though *P. laurocerasus* is intolerant of extreme dryness or alkalinity; pruning not required, but may be clipped to shape in summer or cut back hard in late winter or early spring to limit size or rejuvenate. Propagate from semi-ripe cuttings in early summer.

Pyracantha Firethorn

❝ *Arguably, pyracanthas are the best shrubs for yellow or orange winter fruits and have the advantage that, provided you select the more compact varieties, they can be trained most attractively to geometric two-dimensional shapes against walls. There are, nonetheless, two drawbacks: birds are as attracted to the fruit almost as much as we are; and many varieties, in particular the older ones, are very prone to a disfiguring scab disease. Among those that I recommend, 'Mohave', 'Navaho' and 'Teton' seem fairly resistant.* ❞

WINTER APPEAL Masses of orange or red fruits and evergreen foliage in varying shades.
PERIOD OF WINTER INTEREST Autumn to early winter.
VALUE FOR REST OF THE YEAR Clusters of mustily-scented white or cream flowers in early summer, very attractive to bees.
SIZE 2 x 1.2m (6½ x 4ft) after five years, 4 x 3m (13 x 10ft) after 20 years.

CULTIVATION NOTES
Very hardy, tolerating -20°C (-4°F) or below, though foliage may be damaged by extreme cold; full sun to deep shade, but less fruitful in shade, thrives in any soil except extremely alkaline; pruning not required, but may be cut back in late winter or early spring if necessary; and of course must be pruned to obtain formal, geometric shapes. Propagate from semi-ripe cuttings in early summer.

Pyracantha 'Orange Glow'

Rhododendron

" Despite what you might read elsewhere, no rhododendron is reliably winter flowering in most areas. But that is no reason to ignore them in winter, for many species have particularly attractive leaves, often with a hairy covering or indumentum. Unfortunately, the species are rather less hardy than the hybrids although I have tried to select the tougher among them. "

Rhododendron dauricum

WINTER APPEAL Glossy evergreen foliage.

PERIOD OF WINTER INTEREST Throughout.

VALUE FOR REST OF THE YEAR Trusses of delicate funnel-shaped, sometimes fragrant flowers in white or shades of pink, mauve and yellow appear in spring.

SIZE Low-growing species may reach only 60 x 60cm (24 x 24in) after five years, 1 x 1.5m (3 x 5ft) after 20 years; medium-growing species average about 1.2 x 1.5m (4 x 5ft) after five years, 3 x 4m (10 x 13ft) after 20 years; others may grow to become trees up to 20m (65ft) high.

CULTIVATION NOTES
Moderately hardy, tolerating -10 to -15°C (14 to 5°F); best in light to medium shade; needs an acidic, organic, moist but well-drained soil; pruning not required but dead-heading improves the appearance. Propagation difficult, but may be achieved by layering.

Recommended varieties
Pyracantha angustifolia has orange-yellow fruits and narrow dark green leaves with grey felted undersides. *P. coccinea* 'Lalandei' has masses of orange-red fruits and dark green leaves; 'Red Column', small red fruits, upright habit. 'Golden Charmer' has bright orange-red fruits, glossy bright green leaves arching habit. 'Mohave', especially long-lasting red fruits and dark green leaves. 'Navaho' has orange-red fruits, low growing. 'Orange Glow' has masses of long-lasting orange-red fruits, glossy dark green leaves. *P. rogersiana* has orange-red fruits and narrow, glossy bright green leaves, thrives in shade; 'Flava', bright yellow fruits smaller leaves, weeping; 'Soleil d'Or' has deep yellow fruits, mid- to light green foliage. 'Teton' has orange-yellow fruits and small dark green leaves. 'Watereri' has bright red fruits and dark green leaves.

Recommended varieties
R. cinnabarinum is medium-size with aromatic dark green leaves with a metallic grey-green sheen, and scaly undersides. *R. dauricum* is low-growing and closest to reliably winter flowering with pink flowers in very early spring. *R. griersonianum* is medium with bristly shoots, olive-green leaves with a brown indumentum on the undersides. *R. impeditum* is dwarf with tiny aromatic grey-green scaly leaves. *R. lepidostylum* is dwarf with bristly shoots and small glaucous leaves with golden scaly undersides and hairy margins. *R. yakushimanum* is low and the young leaves are covered with a cinnamon-coloured indumentum, maturing to a glossy dark green with a red-brown indumentum beneath. Species with colourful peeling bark include: *R. barbatum*, tall, red-purple; *R. fulgens*, medium, pink-grey to red-brown; *R. thomsonii*, medium, purple-brown.

SHRUBS

Rosmarinus Rosemary

" *Rosemary is one of gardening's undervalued shrubs. It is, of course, an indispensable herb; but it also makes a quite splendid low hedge if regularly and closely clipped. And it is a valuable evergreen for winter appeal too, either in its neatly clipped state or in the loose straggly but distinctive shape that old specimens tend to adopt.* "

WINTER APPEAL Aromatic grey-green evergreen foliage.
PERIOD OF WINTER INTEREST Throughout.
VALUE FOR REST OF THE YEAR Small blue flowers in spring or early summer.
SIZE Most forms will reach their maximum size of about 1.5 x 1.5m (5 x 5ft) after five to seven years.

CULTIVATION NOTES
Moderately hardy, tolerating -10 to -15°C (14 to 5°F); best in full sun but tolerates light shade; best in light, open, well-drained soil and intolerant of high alkalinity; cut back the oldest one-third of the shoots to soil level in spring to promote new growth; propagate from semi-ripe cuttings in early summer.

Recommended varieties
R. officinalis has narrow grey-green leaves with white undersides, and pale to mid-blue flowers; 'Aureus', yellow markings on the leaves; 'Miss Jessup's Upright', vigorous, taller; and 'Prostratus' is low-growing and less hardy.

Rosmarinus officinalis

Rubus Bramble

" *Winter is very often the season when gardeners spend a good deal of time chopping down brambles. But do not let this struggle against the native species put you off some of its more civilised relatives. For the genus* Rubus *includes the best of all plants for dramatic white stems and also one red-stemmed species that looks spectacular in the low winter sun* "

WINTER APPEAL Brightly-coloured stems in deciduous forms; glossy evergreen foliage in others.
PERIOD OF WINTER INTEREST Throughout.
VALUE FOR REST OF THE YEAR Attractive foliage; flowers in summer followed by fruits that may be edible.
SIZE 1 x 1m (3 x 3ft) after five years, 3 x 3m (10 x10ft) after 20 years, though *R. tricolor* is a ground-cover form with a maximum height of 50cm (20in).

CULTIVATION NOTES
Very hardy, tolerating -20°C (-4°F) or below although foliage can be rather seriously browned by cold winds; tolerates full sun to deep shade, though *R. tricolor* is best in medium shade and deciduous forms look better in full sun; any soil; deciduous forms should be cut back completely to soil level in spring to ensure the production of new stems for winter appeal. Propagate by semi-ripe cuttings in early summer, or by removal of suckers.

Recommended varieties

R. biflorus has brilliant white stems covered with hairy prickles, white felted leaves, small white flowers and yellow edible fruits. I always think this is one of the winter garden's most dramatic plants. *R. cockburnianus* has white stems tinged with purple, fern-like leaves that are dark green-grey above, white beneath, small pink-purple flowers and black fruits with a blue bloom. *R. phoenicolasius* (Wineberry) has bristly red-orange arching stems, small edible orange fruits. *R. thibetanus* has purple-brown stems covered in a white bloom, fern-like, hairy grey-white foliage, small purple flowers and black fruits. *R. tricolor,* effective ground cover, although prone to be severly browned in very cold winter and becomes rather untidy in consequence, has bristly red stems, deeply veined glossy dark green evergreen leaves tinged with red, with white felted undersides, white flowers and sometimes bright red edible fruits.

Rubus cockburnianus 'Golden Vale'

Ruscus Butcher's broom

❝ By no stretch of anyone's imagination is the butcher's broom a spectacular or stunningly beautiful plant. But it is different in form and with the winter's frost on its curious stems, it has a rather special appeal. It's also very useful in winter flower arrangements; and it is simplicity it self to grow. ❞

Ruscus aculeatus

WINTER APPEAL Brilliant red cherry-like fruits on female plants if male plants are grown nearby; dark green glossy evergreen spines or 'cladophylls'.

PERIOD OF WINTER INTEREST Autumn to mid-winter.

VALUE FOR REST OF THE YEAR Evergreen stems of distinctive appearance; unlike almost anything else that you are likely to have in your garden.

SIZE 50 x 60cm (20 x 24in) after five years, 1 x 1.2m (3 x 4ft) after 20 years.

CULTIVATION NOTES

Very hardy, tolerating -20°C (-4°F) or below; needs medium to deep shade; any soil, even if very dry; pruning not required. Propagate by suckers.

Recommended varieties

The normal species, *R. aculeatus* is the most popular form, offering valuable ground cover for a shady site.

SHRUBS

Salix Willow

❝ *What a wonderful genus Salix is. Among its 300 species and numerous varieties is a shrub or tree for every garden. There is no more welcome sign of spring than the first of the 'pussy willow' catkins but there is much to admire in the winter months from the stems, buds and overall appearance and habit of the plants which ranges from the prostrate and creeping to the boldly and vigorously upright.* ❞

WINTER APPEAL Brightly coloured winter stems, buds, and very attractive and distinctive catkins often appearing before the leaves.
PERIOD OF WINTER INTEREST Early winter to spring.
VALUE FOR REST OF THE YEAR Overall shape and habit and/or handsome foliage.
SIZE Varies enormously, from dwarf or prostrate forms that may reach only 15cm x 1m (6in x 3ft) after five years, to medium-sized shrubs that will attain 1-1.5 x 2m (3-5 x 6½ft) after the same time, and very vigorous forms such as *S. alba vitelina* and *S. daphnoides* which, if unpruned, would reach 4 x 1.5m (13 x 5ft) in five years and 6 x 4m (20 x 13ft) or more eventually.

CULTIVATION NOTES
Very hardy, tolerating -20°C (-4°F) or below; thrives in full sun to medium shade, but those with colourful winter stems look best in full sun; any soil, especially if wet or waterlogged; don't prune dwarf and low-growing forms or those grown for their weeping or twisted habit; those grown for their winter stems produce more colourful new shoots if cut back to 30cm (12in) above soil level in early spring every three years. Propagate by hardwood cuttings in winter, by layers or suckers.

Recommended varieties
S. alba vitellina has bright yellow winter shoots, yellow male catkins, yellow-green female catkins in spring; 'Britzensis', orange to red winter shoots; *S. babylonica pekinensis* 'Tortuosa' is fast growing with distinctive twisted branches, bright green twisted leaves and yellow-green catkins. *S. caprea* 'Kilmarnock' is weeping with yellow-brown shoots, grey male catkins on bare stems in spring. *S. daphnoides* (Violet willow) is vigorous with purple shoots covered in winter with a white bloom, grey catkins on bare stems in late winter to early spring; 'Aglaia', shiny red shoots; *S. fargesii* is medium-size with dark red buds in winter, green young shoots in spring that later turn red-brown, and green catkins in spring. *S. hastata* 'Wehrhahnii' is small and slow-growing, with dark purple-brown shoots, bright green leaves and silvery catkins on bare stems in spring. *S. helvetica* is a small, slow-growing shrub bearing golden buds on bare stems in winter that open into silvery-grey catkins, and grey-green leaves. *S. repens* is a prostrate shrub with grey male catkins with golden anthers borne upright on bare stems in early spring. *S. udensis* 'Sekka' is vigorous, with flattened (fastigiate) purple-red stems, sometimes curled at the tips, and silver catkins that appear before the purple-green leaves.

Salix daphnoides 'Aglaia'

Santolina Cotton Lavender

❝ *Santolina is perhaps best known today for its bright yellow summer flowers in the herb garden or flower border. These Mediterranean plants have been grown in our gardens since the sixteenth century, however, as much for their herbal value and striking, feathery white or silver foliage. And this is where their winter appeal lies although they must have friendly conditions to survive without frost damage.* ❞

Santolina chamaecyparissus

WINTER APPEAL Finely divided silver-grey evergreen foliage.

PERIOD OF WINTER INTEREST Throughout.

VALUE FOR REST OF THE YEAR Constant foliage interest; bright yellow flowers in midsummer.

SIZE Reaches its maximum size of about 50 x 75cm (20 x 20in) after two years, and will probably need to be replaced after five.

CULTIVATION NOTES

Fairly hardy, tolerating -5 to -10°C (23 to 14°F) but the foliage will blacken unattractively in cold or wet places; best in full sun or very light shade; must have a light, well-drained soil; prune lightly with shears in late spring to just above the base of last year's growth. propagate by semi-ripe cuttings in summer.

Recommended varieties
S. chamaecyparissus is the most popular form, with grey-white foliage and bright yellow flowers; 'Lambrook Silver' has more silvery leaves.

Sarcococca Christmas Box

❝ *What a name for a winter plant, at least if you garden in the northern hemisphere. Unlike many plants that borrow another plant's name, moreover, they are indeed close relatives of* Buxus, *the true box. They share its evergreen foliage but where they really score is in their small, generally very fragrant flowers.* ❞

WINTER APPEAL Very fragrant flowers and glossy evergreen foliage.

PERIOD OF WINTER INTEREST Throughout.

VALUE FOR REST OF THE YEAR Constant foliage interest; black fruits follow flowers.

SIZE Most forms will reach about 50 x 30cm (20 x 12in) after five years, 2 x 2m ($6^1/_2$ x $6^1/_2$ft) after 20 years, but *S. saligna* may be only half reach twice this size.

CULTIVATION NOTES

Moderately hardy, tolerating -10 to -15°C (14 to 5°F); thrives in full sun to medium shade; needs an organic, fertile soil but tolerates acidity and alkalinity; pruning not required. Propagate by semi-ripe cuttings in late summer, hardwood cuttings in winter.

Recommended varieties
S. confusa has very dark green glossy foliage, white flowers and black fruits. *S. hookeriana digyna* is lower-growing with narrow, rather dull green leaves, pink-tinged flowers and black fruits; *humilis,* also lower-growing, glossy dark green leaves, pink-tinged flowers and blue-black fruits. *S. ruscifolia* has ovate glossy dark green leaves, creamy-white flowers and red fruits. *S. saligna* has narrow, dark green leaves that are paler beneath, unscented green-white flowers and purple fruits.

Sarcococca hookeriana digyna

SHRUBS

Skimmia

Skimmias are undoubtedly very popular and must be among the biggest selling garden shrubs. Yet so many people seem to have problems with them; either because of the insipid looking foliage or the lack of fruits. The latter is generally resolved by choosing additional plants; the former by having a more appropriate soil.

WINTER APPEAL Handsome aromatic evergreen foliage (though rather prone to yellowing) and, on female and hermaphrodite plants, brightly coloured fruits.
PERIOD OF WINTER INTEREST Throughout.
VALUE FOR REST OF THE YEAR Fragrant white flowers in inflorescences in spring; constant foliage interest.
SIZE 40 x 40cm (16 x 16in) after five years, 1 x 1m (3 x 3ft) after 20 years.

CULTIVATION NOTES
Hardy, tolerating -15 to -20°C (5 to -4°F); full sun to medium shade; needs acid to neutral soil, intolerant of alkalinity (which significantly increases the leaf yellowing) or extremely wet or dry conditions. In truth, not easy plants to satisfy; pruning not required. Propagate by semi-ripe cuttings in midsummer, by layering or by removal of suckers.

Recommended varieties
S. x confusa 'Kew Green' is male with mid-green leaves, cream-white flowers. *S. japonica* has dark green leaves, pink- or red-tinged flowers that open from red buds, and, on female plants, red fruit; it has many male and female varieties including: 'Bowles Dwarf', male and female forms are available, compact, red flower-buds in winter; 'Bronze Knight', male, dark red buds; 'Fragrans', male, flowers profusely; 'Nymans', female, larger leaves and bright red fruits; *reevesiana*, hermaphrodite, narrow leaves and rich red fruits; 'Rubella', male, very popular and a lovely plant despite the lack of fruits, with most striking dark red flower buds in winter and red-edged leaves; 'Wakehurst White', female, white fruits.

Skimmia japonica 'Rubella'

Stephanandra

Stephanandra incisa 'Crispa' is a personal crusade plant; one that I have been encouraging people to grow ever since I first discovered it myself. There are few more attractive and striking really hardy deciduous ground-cover shrubs yet, unlike so many ground cover species, it never gets out of hand. And it is one of those rarities that appeals as much with its mass of bare winter stems as it does when clothed with summer foliage.

Stephanandra incisa 'Crispa'

WINTER APPEAL Rich autumn foliage colour, then attractive stems.
PERIOD OF WINTER INTEREST Throughout.
VALUE FOR REST OF THE YEAR Attractive, small hawthorn-like foliage; inflorescences of white flowers in summer.
SIZE S. i. 'Crispa' is a ground-cover plant that will reach only 50 x 75cm (20 x 30in) after five years and 1-1.5 x 1-1.5m (3-5 x 3-5ft) after 20 years; S. tanakae will reach about 1.5 x 1.5m (5 x 5ft) after five years, 3 x 3m (10 x 10ft) after 20 years.

CULTIVATION NOTES

Very hardy, tolerating -20°C (-4°F) or below; tolerates full sun to medium shade, but winter stems appear to best advantage in full sun; does best in rich, fertile soil; not necessary to prune S. incisa 'Crispa', but S. tanakae should have the oldest one-third of the flowering shoots cut back to soil level in spring each year to encourage new growth. Propagate by semi-ripe cuttings in early summer, hardwood cuttings in winter or, with S. i. 'Crispa', removal of suckers or natural layers.

Recommended varieties
S. incisa 'Crispa' has toothed, lobed leaves that turn orange and yellow in autumn, masses of green-white flowers and a dense mass of bright brown winter stems. S. tanakae has similar leaves that turn yellow in autumn, green-white flowers and mahogany winter stems.

Ulex Gorse

" I have never understood why gorse isn't a much more common garden plant. Every time I see masses of it growing wild I find myself exclaiming with pleasure at the sight. I suspect that if someone marketed it as a rare plant from the Himalayas, gardeners would flock to pay handsomely for the privilege of owning one. Because it is a relatively common native species, however, it is passed over. "

WINTER APPEAL Dark green stems and bright yellow flowers that appear intermittently throughout the year.
PERIOD OF WINTER INTEREST Throughout.
VALUE FOR REST OF THE YEAR Dark green spiny stems provide interesting texture and useful screening.
SIZE 80cm x 1m (32in x 3ft) after five years, 2.5 x 4m (8 x 13ft) after 20 years.

CULTIVATION NOTES

Moderately hardy, tolerating -10 to -15°C (14 to 5°F), thrives in coastal conditions, but may be damaged by cold winds; needs full sun to light shade and some shelter; prefers neutral to acid soil but tolerates mild alkalinity; pruning not required. Propagate by semi-ripe cuttings in summer or hardwood cuttings in winter.

Recommended varieties
U. europaeus bears its golden pea-like flowers mainly in late spring to early summer, but they may continue for a much longer period, followed by dark brown seed pods; 'Flore Pleno' is a lower-growing form with double, lemon-yellow flowers.

Ulex europaeus

SHRUBS

Viburnum

" *There are over 150 species of Viburnum and numerous varieties. It is a huge and hugely important genus of deciduous and evergreen shrubs, closely related, perhaps surprisingly, to honeysuckle. But if there is one time of year when this striking group of plants really comes into its own, it happens in the winter garden where, by contributing either foliage or fragrant flowers, they simultaneously add both interest and beauty. Nonetheless, I find viburnums strangely impersonal plants. While the bald facts spell out their virtues, I can't really imagine anyone having a collection of them. I would prefer that most gardens contain at least one representative somewhere.* "

WINTER APPEAL A huge range of varieties, some with masses of fragrant flowers in winter, some with glossy evergreen foliage, while others have autumn foliage colour and attractive fruits.

PERIOD OF WINTER INTEREST Throughout.

VALUE FOR REST OF THE YEAR Prolific spring or summer flowers in some varieties.

SIZE Most forms will reach about 1.5 x 1m (5 x 3ft) after five years and 3-5 x 3-4m (10-16 x 10x13ft) after 20 years, but *V. carlesii* may reach only 2 x 2m (6 1/2 x 6 1/2ft) maximum.

CULTIVATION NOTES

Most forms are very hardy, tolerating -20°C (-4°F) or below, though some spring-flowering forms such as *V. car-* *lesii* are only moderately hardy, tolerating -10 to -15°C (14 to 5°F); best in light shade but tolerates full sun and medium shade; almost any soil; pruning not required; propagate by semi-ripe cuttings in early summer or hardwood cuttings in winter.

Viburnum x bodnantense 'Dawn'

Recommended varieties

V. bodnantense is one of the very best among larger winter-flowering deciduous shrubs with clusters of fragrant, pink-tinged flowers on bare stems from late autumn to early spring; among its most popular varieties are: 'Charles Lamont', bright pink flowers; 'Dawn', dark pink flowers fading to white; and 'Deben', white flowers that open from pink buds. *V. x burkwoodii*, semi-evergreen, includes varieties 'Anne Russell', tending to be more consistently deciduous, very fragrant white flowers opening from pink buds in spring followed by red fruits that ripen to black; 'Park Farm Hybrid', dark pink spring flowers that fade to white followed by red fruits

that later turn black, and glossy green foliage that turns partly orange and red in autumn. *V. carlesii* 'Aurora' is deciduous with pink flowers opening from red buds in spring, followed by red fruits that ripen to black, and dark green toothed leaves that may turn red in autumn. *V. farreri* is deciduous with clusters of fragrant pink or white flowers borne on bare stems in late autumn through winter, followed by bright red fruits, and dark green leaves that are bronze when young and later turn red-purple; 'Candidissimum', deciduous, white flowers, pale yellow fruit and pale green young leaves. *V. japonicum*, evergreen, has fragrant white flowers in early summer, bright red

fruit and glossy dark green leaves. *V. opulus* (Guelder rose) is deciduous with flat lace-cap white flowerheads surrounded by ray-florets in early summer, bright red fruits, and maple-like leaves that turn red in autumn. *V. tinus* is evergreen, with clusters of white flowers in late winter and spring, blue-black fruits and dark green leaves; among its finest varieties are: 'Eve Price', pink flower buds; 'Gwenllian', masses of dark pink buds and pink-flushed flowers; 'Lucidum', very vigorous, glossy leaves and larger flowers; 'Purpureum', whose young foliage is bronze-purple; and 'Variegatum', cream-yellow-edged leaves.

WINTER APPEAL Attractive evergreen, often variegated, ground-cover foliage.
PERIOD OF WINTER INTEREST Throughout.
VALUE FOR REST OF THE YEAR Bright blue, white or purple flowers in spring to summer.
SIZE *V. major* will reach its maximum size of about 40cm x 1m (16in x 3ft) after five years, and *V. minor* about 15 x 80cm (6 x 32in) in the same time.

CULTIVATION NOTES

Very hardy, tolerating -20°C (-4°F) or below; best in light shade but tolerates full sun and medium shade; almost any soil, even if very dry; every two or three years in spring *V. major* should be cut back to soil level with shears or powered trimmer, and *V. minor* trimmed lightly, to produce strong new growth. Propagate by semi-ripe cuttings in early summer, hardwood cuttings in winter, or by removal of naturally rooted layers.

Recommended varieties
V. major has dark green glossy foliage and bright blue star-shaped flowers from mid-spring to mid-summer; 'Variegata', large, cream-edged leaves and pale blue flowers. *V. minor* has smaller leaves and purple-blue flowers; among its most attractive varieties are: 'Alba Variegata', white flowers and yellow-edged leaves; 'Argenteovariegata', pale violet flowers and creamy-white-edged leaves; 'Atropurpurea', dark purple flowers; 'Gertrude Jekyll', profuse white flowers; and 'La Grave', lavender-blue flowers.

Viburnum opulus

Vinca Periwinkle

❝ *I don't know how I could garden without* Vinca. *One or other of the varieties clothes the ground in most of the dry, slightly shaded areas of my garden. It's on to them that the leaves fall from the deciduous trees in autumn and it's through them that the first of the spring-flowering bulbs push their heads. They truly form a carpet for all seasons.* ❞

Vinca minor 'Argenteovariegata'

TREES – NON-CONIFERS

Amelanchier Snowy Mespilus

" As regular readers will know, this is the tree without which I could not garden. It is the small-garden tree for all seasons and all places; which is precisely why I have one in arguably the prime spot in my entire garden, to greet visitors as they enter the main gate. Its virtues can be summed up as a combination of all season attractiveness (the one slight difficulty being that the fruit sometimes don't give the display that they should because they are much loved by blackbirds) and an ability to tolerate almost any soil. "

WINTER APPEAL Brilliant foliage colours and attractive fruits in autumn; delicate tracery of twigs when leaves have dropped.
PERIOD OF WINTER INTEREST Autumn to early winter.
VALUE FOR REST OF THE YEAR Masses of delicate white blossom in spring; delicately pretty summer foliage.
SIZE 3 x 1.5m (10 x 5ft) after five years, 8 x 3m (25 x 10ft) after 20 years.

CULTIVATION NOTES
Very hardy, tolerating -20°C (-4°F) or below; best in full sun but tolerates medium shade and strong winds; any soil, even heavy clay; pruning not required, but to form a single-stemmed tree, cut away any suckers that may arise at the base. Propagate from rooted suckers or hardwood cuttings.

Recommended varieties
Amelanchier lamarckii. A plant generally called *A. canadensis* is inferior and much more prone to sucker.

Amelanchier lamarckii

Betula Birch

" Every year, but most especially every winter, I say a little 'thank you' to the unknown previous owner of my garden who, some 30 years ago, planted a white-barked Himalayan birch outside what is now my office window. Like so many of its kin, it has naturally divided below soil level to form a twin-trunked tree of surpassing loveliness when the low winter sun strikes that exquisite white bark. And I am reminded of it wherever else in the garden I go, for pieces of the bark flake off and blow around like pieces of natural waste-paper. "

WINTER APPEAL Beautiful bare stems, white or attractively patterned; sometimes with peeling bark.
PERIOD OF WINTER INTEREST Throughout.
VALUE FOR REST OF THE YEAR Catkins in spring, autumn foliage colour.
SIZE About 6 x 1.5m (20 x 5ft) after five years, 12 x 5m (40 x 16ft) after 20 years.

CULTIVATION NOTES
Very hardy, tolerating -20°C (-4°C) or below; tolerates light shade but prefers, and looks best in, full sun; almost any soil except waterlogged, but does better in slightly acid than slightly alkaline conditions; pruning not required except to remove unwanted lower branches. Propagate by grafting.

Recommended varieties

Betula albosinensis (Chinese red birch) has distinctive orange-brown peeling bark, covered in a white bloom when young, yellow-brown male catkins, and glossy dark green leaves that turn yellow in autumn. The following Asiatic and Himalayan white-barked birches are not easy to differentiate but are equally beautiful: *B. ermanii* (Erman's birch) has pink-cream bark, yellow-brown male catkins and dark green leaves that turn yellow in autumn. *B. utilis* has peeling copper-brown or pink bark, dark green leaves that turn yellow in autumn, yellow-brown male catkins; *jacquemontii*, pure white stems and brown patches of peeling bark, masses of catkins and good yellow if brief autumn foliage colour; 'Jermyns' is the commonest of several selected forms.

Hamamelis Witch Hazel

❝ Witch hazels can be fickle things. If they don't take a liking to your soil, they will sulk and flower feebly. But give them their ideal spot (which I still think is with a little shelter and a little acidity), and their late-winter flowers will offer infallible evidence that there is life after the frost. I know of few other shrubs that so repay thorough and careful soil preparation; or are so averse to being moved once established. But if all else fails and they still let you down, do as pre-nineteenth century gardeners did and grow Cornus mas (page 21) instead. ❞

Recommended varieties

Hamamelis x *intermedia* appears as many fine varieties, all bearing fragrant flowers, including: 'Arnold Promise', large yellow flowers; 'Diane', dark red flowers and yellow, orange and red autumn foliage; 'Jelena', copper-orange flowers and orange and red autumn foliage; 'Pallida', sulphur-yellow flowers; and 'Sunburst', large pale yellow flowers. *H. mollis* (Chinese witch hazel) bears very fragrant golden-yellow flowers, and has mid-green leaves that turn yellow in autumn; 'Coombe Wood' is a more spreading plant with large, very fragrant flowers.

WINTER APPEAL Clusters of yellow, gold, red or brown spidery flowers, sometimes fragrant, borne on bare stems.
PERIOD OF WINTER INTEREST Mid-winter to spring.
VALUE FOR REST OF THE YEAR Autumn foliage colour.
SIZE Slow-growing at first, reaching about 1.5 x 1.5m (5 x 5ft) after five years, 5 x 4m (16 x 13ft) after 20 years.

CULTIVATION NOTES

Hardy to very hardy, tolerating about -20°C (-4°F) but prone to damage by cold winds when flowers are open so best in a sheltered position; best in full sun or light shade; prefers neutral to acid, organic, free-draining soil; pruning not required. Propagate by layers.

Betula utilis jaquemontii

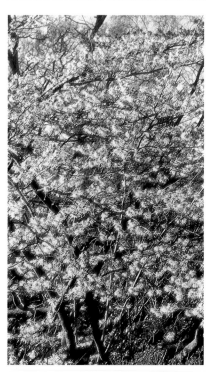

Hamamelis x *intermedia* 'Pallida'

Ilex Holly

❝ *The Christmas plant par exellence, but a fine tree for the rest of the year too. Don't be conservative in your choice as the range is now enormous; and never forget that many of the loveliest varieties are yellow- not red-fruited.* ❞

WINTER APPEAL Brilliantly coloured fruits; glossy, evergreen, sometimes variegated foliage.
PERIOD OF WINTER INTEREST Throughout.
VALUE FOR REST OF THE YEAR Constant foliage interest.
SIZE The recommended varieties will reach about 3.5 x 1.5m (11 x 5ft) after five years, 6.5 x 3.5m (22 x 11ft) after 20 years.

Ilex aquifolium 'Bacciflava'

CULTIVATION NOTES

Very hardy, tolerating -20°C (-4°F) or below; thrives in full sun to medium shade; any soil, but does best on one that is rich and moist; pruning not required. Can be difficult to propagate but semi-ripe cuttings in summer tend to be more successful than hardwood cuttings in winter. Most forms do not come true from seed.

Recommended varieties
Ilex x altaclarensis 'Belgica Aurea' is female with gold-edged leaves with mottled grey-green centres and few spines, yellow stems, few fruits; 'Golden King', female, gold-edged leaves with mottled grey-green centres and few spines, few red-brown fruits; 'Lawsoniana', female, gold and yellow green-centred leaves, yellow stems, red-brown fruits. *I. aquifolium* 'Argentea Marginata' is female with spiny purple-pink young leaves becoming cream-streaked and white-edged when mature, many bright red fruits; 'Bacciflava', female, spiny dark green leaves and yellow fruits; 'Ferox Argentea', male, very spiny, cream-margined leaves; 'Golden Milkboy', male, spiny gold-centred leaves, purple stems; 'Golden Queen', male, gold-edged leaves, some spines, cream-streaked stems; 'Handsworth New Silver', female, spiny, cream-edged leaves, purple stems, bright red fruits; 'Madame Briot', female, spiny, gold-edged leaves, purple stems, scarlet fruits; 'Silver Milkmaid', female, spiny, silver or white-centred leaves, many scarlet fruits; 'Silver Queen', male, spiny cream-edged leaves, purple stems.

Magnolia grandiflora

❝ *This is a plant that is much hardier than is often imagined. The only drawback I have experienced is that the branches are rather brittle and heavy falls of snow should be knocked off them promptly to prevent them snapping.* ❞

WINTER APPEAL Leathery, glossy evergreen leaves.
PERIOD OF WINTER INTEREST Throughout.
VALUE FOR REST OF THE YEAR Very fragrant, large cream-white flowers from late summer to autumn; constant foliage interest.
SIZE 3 x 1m (10 x 3ft) after five years, 8 x 4m (25 x 13ft) after 20 years.

CULTIVATION NOTES

Fairly hardy, tolerating -5 to -10°C (23 to 14°F); thrives in full sun to medium shade, often trained against a wall to give shelter in exposed gardens although it also makes a fine free-standing tree; thrives in most soils but best in a deep, organic, acid to neutral loam; pruning not required. Propagate by semi-ripe cuttings in early summer.

Recommended varieties
Magnolia grandiflora 'Exmouth' is hardier than other forms, flowers earlier in its life, and has dark green leaves with brown felted undersides; 'Goliath', very large flowers that appear three to five years after planting, and lighter, twisted leaves.

Malus Crab Apple

66 *Crab apples are very good small garden trees. Sadly, they generally fail as winter plants because birds remove the fruit long before the cold weather sets in. The one exception is 'Golden Hornet' and I commend it very warmly.* 99

WINTER APPEAL Brightly coloured, long-lasting fruits.
PERIOD OF WINTER INTEREST Autumn to mid-winter.
VALUE FOR REST OF THE YEAR White blossom in spring.
SIZE 4 x 1.5m (13 x 5ft) after five years, 8 x 6m (25 x 20ft) after 20 years.

CULTIVATION NOTES
Moderately hardy, tolerating -10 to -15°C (14 to 4°F); best in full sun to very light shade; almost any soil, but dislikes heavy, wet clay; pruning not required except to remove damaged or crossing branches in winter. Impossible to propagate by cuttings.

Malus 'Golden Hornet'

Recommended varieties
Malus 'Golden Hornet' has masses of golden-yellow fruits that last well into winter, has white flowers opening from pink buds and toothed, bright green leaves.

Prunus Flowering Cherry

66 *You may or may not like the spring-blooming ornamental cherries. But you can hardly fail to be attracted to their few relatives that either bloom in the winter or offer other appealing cold-weather features. One word of caution: the winter-flowering cherry, so often recommended for small gardens, will become a big plant rather sooner than you expect.* 99

WINTER APPEAL Flowers in some varieties; shiny, colourful peeling bark in others.
PERIOD OF WINTER INTEREST Throughout.
VALUE FOR REST OF THE YEAR Autumn foliage colour; spring blossom in some varieties.
SIZE About 3-4 x 2-3m (10-13 x 6-10ft) after five years, 7-8 x 6-8m (23-25 x 20-25ft) after 20 years. Beyond this age they soon begin to decline through disease.

CULTIVATION NOTES
Very hardy, tolerating -20°C (-4°F) or below; full sun to very light shade; almost any soil, but intolerant of heavy, wet clay; pruning not required except to remove damaged or crossing branches in winter. Very hard to propagate by cuttings.

Recommended varieties
Prunus 'Mount Fuji' has dark green leaves that turn orange and red in autumn, and fragrant single or semi-double white flowers. *P. serrula* has peeling, shiny, red-brown bark, dark green leaves that turn yellow in autumn, white flowers, red, cherry-like fruits. *P.* x *subhirtella* 'Autumnalis' has semi-double pink-tinged white flowers during mild periods from autumn to spring, sometimes followed by red cherry-like fruits that later turn black, leaves that are bronze when young and yellow in autumn; 'Autumnalis Rosea', similar but with pink flowers.

Prunus subhirtella 'Autumnalis Rosea'

TREES – CONIFERS

Abies Silver Fir

❝ If you have space, then the silver firs will make the most splendid specimen trees. Sadly, few of us have gardens large enough to accommodate them but, fortunately, to the rescue comes the Korean fir. This lovely tree not only produces cones at a younger age than any other conifer that I know, it also has cones that are among the most beautiful in the conifer kingdom. ❞

WINTER APPEAL Shiny dark green evergreen leaves with silver undersides.
PERIOD OF WINTER INTEREST Throughout.
VALUE FOR REST OF THE YEAR Shape, texture and colour provide constant interest; colourful cones in late spring and early summer.
SIZE A. koreana is smaller than most, reaching about 1.5 x 1m (5 x 3ft) after five years and 12 x 6m (40 x 20ft) after 20 years. Don't make the mistake, however, of thinking this a dwarf species: it isn't, it is merely a slow-growing one.

CULTIVATION NOTES

Very hardy, tolerating -20°C (-4°F) or below, though new foliage may be damaged by frost; best in an open site in full sun but with some shelter from winds; prefers deep, well-drained, neutral to acid soil; do not prune. Almost impossible to propagate by cuttings.

Recommended varieties

Abies koreana (Korean fir) is particularly slow-growing when young, but starts to bear its purple-blue cones when only about 1m (3ft) tall; 'Silberlocke' has twisted leaves that reveal their silver undersides.

Abies koreana

Cedrus Cedar

❝ Cedars are for big gardens but for the benefit of gardeners who do have the space, I have included the best varieties here. Even if you have a good deal of room, I would still warn you off the Cedar of Lebanon (and its close relative, the Deodar). This tree truly needs a stately home and stately grounds to look right. And be aware, too, that all cedars are prone to damage by gales or heavy snow falls when the top can be snapped. On more than one occasion, I have been called in to advise on liability when a large branch has deposited itself on a house following damage to a tree that had been planted too close to the building. ❞

WINTER APPEAL Evergreen foliage; majestic habit.
PERIOD OF WINTER INTEREST Throughout.
VALUE FOR REST OF THE YEAR Shape, texture and colour provide constant interest; attractive cones in autumn.
SIZE About 8 x 3m (25 x 10ft) after 10 years, 12 x 4m (40 x 13ft) after 20 years, and twice this eventually.

CULTIVATION NOTES

Very hardy, tolerating -20°C (-4°F) or below; best in full sun in a huge open site; almost any soil, but best in a deep, rich, moist loam; do not prune. Almost impossible to propagate by cuttings.

Recommended varieties
Cedrus libani atlantica 'Glauca'
(Blue Atlas cedar) has silver-blue
foliage that is especially bright in
spring, and bears upright cones in
autumn that are green at first, ripening to brown; 'Glauca Pendula, is an
astonishing form; *brevifolia* (Cyprus
cedar) grey- or blue-green foliage,
silver-grey bark and green cones
that ripen to brown.

Cedrus atlanticus **'Glauca Pendula'**

Juniperus Juniper

*❝ The juniper is one of our three native conifers and it is the only
one that doesn't eventually reach a very large size. In truth, the native
species is a rather boring plant but there are several others well worth
garden room; and this is the genus above all that has yielded some quite
excellent dwarf varieties. ❞*

WINTER APPEAL Graceful habit;
evergreen, sometimes aromatic,
foliage; sometimes colourful peeling
bark.
PERIOD OF WINTER INTEREST
Throughout.
VALUE FOR REST OF THE YEAR
Shape, texture and colour provide
constant interest; attractive cones
or fruits.
SIZE Varies enormously with variety: *Juniperus chinensis* 'Aurea' will
reach about 10-15 x 3-4m (33-50 x
10-13ft) eventually, *J. recurva* 'Coxii'
about 15 x 7m (50 x 23ft), and
J. squamata 'Meyeri' 5-7 x 5-7m
(16-23 x 16-23ft). There are also
many very good dwarf varieties.

Juniperus squamata **'Holger'**

CULTIVATION NOTES
Very hardy, tolerating -20°C (-4°F)
or below; full sun to light shade with
shelter from cold winds; best on a
deep, rich, moist loam, but tolerates
most soils even if acid, alkaline or dry;
pruning not advisable. Propagate by
semi-ripe cuttings in early summer or
hardwood cuttings in winter, but may
need misting.

Recommended varieties
J. chinensis 'Aurea' is a tall, narrow,
erect tree with aromatic, golden
foliage, peeling brown bark and
many purple-brown cones in
spring. *J. recurva* 'Coxii' (Coffin
juniper) is a conical form with
pendulous dark green foliage, flaky
orange-brown bark and fleshy black
fruit. *J. squamata* 'Meyeri' is a
spreading tree with blue-green
foliage, flaky brown bark and glossy
black fruit.

TREES – CONIFERS

Cypresses

❝ The cypresses are the most widely planted garden conifers. From a handful of mainly North American species have come varieties to conquer the gardening world. But unfortunately, many are planted for functional rather than aesthetic reasons and, in consequence, some rather dull plants have given the group a bad name. Choose carefully, and cypresses can beautify the winter garden with their shapes and colours; plant unthinkingly, and your garden may not only dull but dwarfed and shaded too. ❞

Chamaecyparis False Cypress

WINTER APPEAL Evergreen foliage borne in flattened sprays in varying colours; graceful habit.
PERIOD OF WINTER INTEREST Throughout.
VALUE FOR REST OF THE YEAR Shape, texture and colour provide constant interest, whether as specimen trees or as a foil for other plants.
SIZE *Chamaecyparis obtusa* 'Crippsii' and *C. thyoides* will reach only about 10 x 3-5m (33 x 10-16ft) eventually; there are so many varieties of *C. lawsoniana* (see right) that it's almost impossible to generalise. Suffice it to say that the true species will reach 10-15 x 1-3m (33-50 x 3-10ft) eventually but that varieties can be chosen to attain almost all heights below this.

CULTIVATION NOTES
Very hardy, tolerating -20°C (-4°F) or below; best in full sun; prefers a moist, well-drained neutral to acid soil, but tolerates some alkalinity; hedging may be trimmed from late spring to early autumn, but hard pruning is inadvisable, as it will not regenerate from old wood. Can be propagated by semi-ripe cuttings in early spring but this isn't easy without a misting facility.

Chamaecyparis lawsoniana

Recommended varieties
There are more varieties of *C. lawsoniana* (Lawson cypress) than of any other cultivated tree. In Britain alone, there were well over 200 available when last I checked. In large measure, you will be restricted to those that your supplier chooses to stock and the following personal selection is really intended to indicate the scope. They generally have a red-brown scaly bark, bright red male flowers that open from blue-black buds, and red-brown female cones. 'Erecta Viridis', broad with erect branches and a pointed top, bright green foliage; 'Fletcheri' usually forms several pointed columns, with grey foliage that curves upwards; 'Green Pillar', narrow, upright with bright green foliage; 'Kilmacurragh', narrow, bright green foliage; 'Lutea', slow-growing at first, bears its golden foliage in graceful drooping sprays; 'Pembury Blue' is conical, with drooping sprays of aromatic, blue-grey foliage; 'Pottenii' has feathery yellow-green foliage; 'Stewartii' is conical, with distinctive narrow sprays of brilliant golden foliage, an excellent older variety; 'Wisselii', narrow, conical, with sprays of blue-green foliage and many cones in spring. Among other species, I specially commend the following: *C. nootkatensis* 'Pendula' has long, upward-curving branches draped with aromatic dark green foliage, cones that ripen to brown, and grey-brown bark, sometimes peeling. *C. obtusa* 'Crippsii' is slow-growing with sprays of aromatic, golden foliage, brown cones, and red-brown bark.

Cupressus True Cypress

WINTER APPEAL Graceful habit and striking evergreen foliage colours.
PERIOD OF WINTER INTEREST Throughout.
VALUE FOR REST OF THE YEAR Shape, texture and colour provide constant interest.

SIZE Varies considerably: *Cupressus arizonica* 'Pyramidalis' will reach 10-15 x 4-5m (33-50 x 13-16ft); *C. macrocarpa* 'Gold Crest', probably about 10 x 2.5m (33 x 8ft), and *C. torulosa* 'Cashmeriana' in mild conditions, as much as 30 x 10m (100 x 33ft).

CULTIVATION NOTES

Most forms are very hardy, tolerating -20°C (-4°F) or below, but the beautiful *C. torulosa* 'Cashmeriana' is only fairly hardy, tolerating -5 to -10°C (23 to 14°F); best in full sun with shelter from cold winds; any well-drained soil, whether acid or alkaline; hedges may be trimmed in late spring, but do not prune hard as they won't regenerate from old wood. Propagate by semi-ripe cuttings in early spring although this is difficult without a misting facility.

Recommended varieties

C. arizonica 'Pyramidalis' is broadly conical with blue-green foliage. *C. macrocarpa* 'Gold Crest' is a lovely narrowly conical, lime green-gold form of the Monterey cypress, with aromatic feathery foliage. *C. torulosa* 'Cashmeriana' (Kashmir cypress) is conical when young, spreading when older, with glorious aromatic, drooping sprays of glaucous blue foliage and small dark brown cones.

Cupressus macrocarpa 'Goldcrest'

X Cupressocyparis

WINTER APPEAL Graceful evergreen foliage in a range of colours.
PERIOD OF WINTER INTEREST Throughout.
VALUE FOR REST OF THE YEAR Shape, texture and colour provide constant interest.
SIZE Varies enormously. My recommendation, X *Cupressocyparis leylandii* 'Robinson's Gold' may reach 20 x 4-5m (65 x 13-16ft) eventually although, as with all Leyland cypresses, its true potential for growth has not yet been realised. All green forms grow at a prodigious rate and should be planted only after very careful thought of the consequences. One very distinguished tree expert suggested that within 30 years, much of urban Britain could vanish beneath this species.

CULTIVATION NOTES

Very hardy, tolerating -20°C (-4°F) or below; full sun or medium shade; any deep, well-drained soil; hedges may need to be trimmed two or three times between spring and early autumn, but do not cut into old wood as it will not regenerate. Propagate by semi-ripe cuttings in early spring although this is extremely difficult without a misting facility.

Recommended varieties

x C. l. 'Robinson's Gold' has flattened sprays of bronze-yellow foliage in spring, maturing to gold.

X Cupressocyparis leylandii

Picea Spruce

" *Of course, for most people,* the *winter spruce is* Picea abies, *the Norway spruce or Christmas tree. But please don't make the mistake of thinking it a satisfactory garden plant. Few sights are more depressing than last year's Christmas tree, spindly and struggling in the garden the following autumn. Treat Christmas trees as expendable and choose a more appropriate species for your garden.* "

WINTER APPEAL Graceful habit and evergreen foliage in various colours.
PERIOD OF WINTER INTEREST Throughout.
VALUE FOR REST OF THE YEAR Shape, texture and colour provide constant interest.
SIZE Varies enormously: dwarf forms exist, but most are fast-growing. *P. breweriana* and *P. omorika* will reach 15-20 x 4-5m (50-65 x 13-16ft), *P. orientalis* 30 x 6-8m (100 x 20-25ft).

Picea omorika

CULTIVATION NOTES
Very hardy, tolerating -20°C (-4°F) or below; best in full sun; any deep, moist, well-drained soil, preferably neutral to acid, though *P. omorika* is usefully tolerant of alkalinity; do not prune. Almost impossible to propagate by cuttings.

Recommended varieties
P. breweriana is slow-growing and slender, with glossy dark blue-green foliage on beautiful drooping branches, purple cones. *P. omorika* is elegant and narrow, with upward-curving branches bearing dark blue-green foliage, white beneath, and red-brown cones. *P. orientalis* 'Aurea' has bright yellow foliage in spring, later turning green, with dark red and purple cones.

Pinus Pine

" *When they are good, with long graceful needles or a rich golden colour, pines can be glorious. When they are bad, they are depressing. Choose and position them carefully so their overall shape can be seen to proper advantage. A good pine lost among others trees is a wasted opportunity.* "

WINTER APPEAL Graceful habit and evergreen foliage in various colours; sometimes attractive bark and cones.
PERIOD OF WINTER INTEREST Throughout.
VALUE FOR REST OF THE YEAR Shape, texture and colour provide constant interest.
SIZE Varies enormously; the smallest of my choices, *P. bungeana* and *P. sylvestris* 'Aurea', will reach about 10-15 x 3-4m (33-50 x 10-13ft), the largest, *P. jeffreyi*, about 25-35 x 6-8m (82-115 x 20-25ft), and the rest somewhere in between.

CULTIVATION NOTES
Most are very hardy, tolerating -20°C (-4°F) or below; best in full sun; any well-drained soil, preferably acid to neutral; do not prune. Almost impossible to propagate by cuttings.

Recommended varieties
P. bungeana is slow-growing with grey-green flaking bark revealing cream patches that turn purple, and shiny dark green leaves. *P. jeffreyi* is conical with blue-green leaves and a fissured black bark. *P. leucodermis*, narrowly conical, has dark green foliage, scaly grey bark and bright blue cones that ripen to brown. *P. montezumae* bears tufts of grey-green leaves, yellow-orange cones, and fissured grey-brown bark. *P. sylvestris* 'Aurea' has blue-green foliage, golden-yellow in winter. *P. wallichiana*, conical but later domed, has pendent grey- or blue-green leaves and has a smooth grey bark.

Taxus Yew

" The finest hedging plant of them all; but a lovely specimen tree also. Grow the normal native species if you have room and if you want a dense dark green background for paler coloured things. Grow a golden yew and preferably a fastigiate golden one if your space is more limited. "

WINTER APPEAL Densely beautiful evergreen foliage, dark green or golden.
PERIOD OF WINTER INTEREST Throughout.
VALUE FOR REST OF THE YEAR Shape, texture and colour provide constant interest; vivid red 'fruits' on female trees give added appeal.
SIZE *Taxus baccata* will reach about 2 x 2m (6½ x 6½ft) after 10 years, 4 x 2.5-3m (13 x 8-10ft) after 20 years, and possibly 30 x 20m (100 x 65ft) eventually; its varieties are slower growing: 'Dovastoniana' will reach about 15m (50ft) eventually, 'Fastigiata' about 10 x 4m (33 x 13ft), and 'Fastigiata Aurea' about 6 x 3m (20 x 10ft).

CULTIVATION NOTES
Very hardy, tolerating -20°C (-4°F) or below; full sun to fairly deep shade, and tolerates exposure but may be stunted by constant wind; almost any soil, including very alkaline, but best on a deep, rich loam; pruning not required, but neglected plants will regenerate if cut back hard into old or even very old wood in spring; hedges should be trimmed once in midsummer and again in early autumn. Propagate by semi-ripe cuttings in early spring.

Recommended varieties
T. baccata has horizontal branches, dark green needles, purple-brown bark, yellow male cones in spring and red 'fruits' from late summer; among its finest varieties are: 'Dovastoniana', male, weeping branchlets; 'Fastigiata', female, erect branches; 'Fastigiata Aurea', female, gold-variegated foliage.

Taxus baccata 'Standishii'

Thuja False Cedar

" A wonderful wind-break tree, far more attractive than many a cypress, and a tree that could so usefully take their place in a wide range of situations. One small warning: the foliage can cause an unpleasant skin rash on some people. "

WINTER APPEAL Graceful, aromatic evergreen foliage.
PERIOD OF WINTER INTEREST Throughout.
VALUE FOR REST OF THE YEAR Shape, texture and colour provide constant interest.
SIZE The recommended varieties will reach about 10-15 x 2-4m (33-50 x 6/12-13ft) eventually but respond well to having the tops removed every few years to encourage a more compact habit.

CULTIVATION NOTES
Very hardy, tolerating -20°C (-4°F); best in full sun to light shade, with shelter from cold winds when young; tolerates most soils but best when deep, moist and well-drained; pruning not required, but trim hedges once in midsummer and in early autumn. Propagate by semi-ripe cuttings in spring.

Recommended varieties
Thuja occidentalis 'Spiralis' has twisted, fern-like sprays of aromatic grey-green foliage, and has orange-brown bark and yellow-green cones that ripe to brown. *T. plicata* 'Zebrina' is broadly conical, with flat sprays of peculiar yellow-striped leaves that you will find very attractive or simply loathe, red-brown bark and green cones ripening to brown.

Acaena

" *If a rather loose mat of tiny prickly red beads strikes you as a way of brightening up your winter garden, then the New Zealand bidi-bidi is the genus for you. I am very partial to them (they look delicious with a dusting of snow), but be warned that they can be invasive if not trimmed back regularly.* "

WINTER APPEAL Pretty ever-green ground-cover foliage in vari-ous shades.
PERIOD OF WINTER INTEREST Throughout.
VALUE FOR REST OF THE YEAR Small flowers in summer followed by colourful fruiting burrs.
SIZE Most will attain about 3-5 x 45-60cm (1½-2 x 18-24in) in three years.

Acaena microphylla 'Copper Carpet'

CULTIVATION NOTES

Moderately hardy, tolerating -10 to -15°C (14 to 4°F); full sun to partial shade; most well-drained soils. Limit size of the more vigorous varieties if necessary by cutting off runners which can be used for propagation; also propagate by softwood cuttings in late spring.

Recommended varieties
Acaena microphylla has bronze-green leaves and crimson burrs; 'Kupferteppich', coppery leaves and bright red burrs. *A. novae-zelandiae* has grey-green or rich green leaves and red burrs. *A. saccaticupula* 'Blue Haze' has blue-green leaves, bright red, relatively spine-free burrs.

Adonis

" *I think of* Adonis *as rather grand aconites. They belong to the same family, the Ranunculaceae, as is betrayed by their very similar golden buttercup flowers. But the beautiful frilly 'ruff' of* Adonis *sets it apart and gives them an alto-gether more stylish appearance.* "

WINTER APPEAL Bright yellow buttercup-like flowers borne on bare stems.
PERIOD OF WINTER INTEREST Late winter to spring
VALUE FOR REST OF THE YEAR Delicate fern-like foliage from spring to early summer.
SIZE 20-40 x 30-45cm (8-16 x 12-18in) within two or three years.

CULTIVATION NOTES

Moderately hardy, tolerating -10 to -15°C (14 to 5°F); *A. amurensis* is a woodland species, preferring a shady site with a rich, moist, light acidic soil; *A. vernalis* is better in full sun, with a well-drained, slightly alkaline soil. Propagate by seed, or division after flowering.

Recommended varieties
A. amurensis has bright yellow flowers; 'Flore Pleno', double, green-yellow flowers. *A. vernalis* has golden flowers in spring.

Adonis amurensis

Ajuga

" *Ajugas are good, all-year-round carpeting plants that will attract attention in winter with their rich red or bronze foliage and, later in the year, with their flowers, deep blue in the best forms. Sadly, they will also attract attention because of their mildew in warm dry sum-mers and their tattered and slug browsed leaves in wet winters.* "

WINTER APPEAL Attractive evergreen ground-cover foliage in various colours.
PERIOD OF WINTER INTEREST Throughout.
VALUE FOR REST OF THE YEAR Constant foliage interest; rich blue, pink or white flowers in spring.
SIZE *A. pyramidalis* will reach 15 x 30-40cm (6-12 x 12-16in), but the more vigorous forms of *A. reptans* will spread to 60-90cm (24-34in) or more within about four years.

Right: *Ajuga reptans* 'Burgundy Glow'
Below: *Artemisia caucasica*

CULTIVATION NOTES
Moderately hardy, tolerating -10 to -15°C (14 to 5°F); best in partial or full shade; any moist soil, *A. reptans* will thrive even in very poor soil. Propagate by rooted stems or softwood cuttings in early summer, or by division.

Recommended varieties
A. pyramidalis 'Metallica Crispa' has curled, metallic purple-green leaves and dark blue flowers. *A. reptans* (Bugle) appears in many attractive forms including: 'Atropurpurea', with glossy purple-bronze leaves and dark blue flowers; 'Braunherz', very dark purple leaves and dark blue flowers; 'Burgundy Glow', silver-green leaves tinged with dark red; 'Catlin's Giant', very vigorous, exceptionally large bronze-purple leaves, and taller flowers; 'Multicolor', bronze-green leaves tinged with cream and pink.

Artemisia

❝ At their best, in relatively dry soils and relatively dry weather, artemisias have much to commend them with their delicate fern-like foliage and the intense silver tints of the best forms. In cold wet winters, sadly, they do tend to turn black, brown and other less savoury shades and then look thoroughly miserable. They must be cut back hard in spring to rejuvenate them. ❞

WINTER APPEAL Delicate silver-grey foliage, often aromatic.
PERIOD OF WINTER INTEREST Throughout.
VALUE FOR REST OF THE YEAR Constant foliage interest; yellow flowerheads in late summer.
SIZE *Artemisia abrotanum, A. arborescens* and *A. ludoviciana* will form clumps about 1 x 1m (3 x 3ft) within about four years, the other recommended varieties about two-thirds this size, except for *A. s.* 'Nana', which will reach only about 8 x 30cm (3½ x 12in).

CULTIVATION NOTES
Most artemisia are moderately hardy, tolerating -10 to -15°C (14 to 5°F), but *A. arborescens* needs the shelter of a warm wall in cold areas and all varieties can blacken in cold winters; grow in full sun; any well-drained, fertile soil; cut back hard in autumn. Propagate by seed or division.

Recommended varieties
A. abrotanum (Southernwood) has deciduous or semi-evergreen, aromatic feathery grey leaves. *A. absinthium* 'Lambrook Silver', evergreen with aromatic, deeply divided silver-grey leaves. *A. arborescens*, evergreen with aromatic, fern-like silver-white leaves; *A. ludoviciana*, evergreen with lance-shaped, downy silver-white leaves and woolly flowerheads; 'Valerie Finnis', deeply cut silver-grey leaves. *A.* 'Powis Castle' has evergreen feathery silver-grey leaves. *A. schmidtiana* has semi-evergreen tufts of fine, silky grey-green leaves; 'Nana' is similar but smaller.

Bergenia Elephant's Ears

   ❝ *Bergenias have long been classed as 'useful' plants; which essentially means that they are relatively attractive but will never be stars of the border. Dear Miss Jekyll knew their worth and used them extensively in some of her best known gardens. And so should you in yours; but plant them where their winter value can be seen to best advantage.* ❞

Bergenia 'Abendglut'

flowers in extreme cold; thrives in full sun or partial shade; any soil, even heavy clay, and winter foliage colours are stronger in poorer soil. Propagate by division in autumn or spring.

Recommended varieties

Bergenia 'Bressingham Ruby' has deep red-purple leaves, deep red flowers. *B. cordifolia* 'Purpurea' has dark purple-green leaves, deep pink flowers. *B. purpurascens* has dark green leaves that turn purple or red in winter, purple-red flowers. *B. x schmidtii* has mid-green, toothed leaves, clear pink flowers. *B.* 'Sunningdale' has mid-green leaves that turn red in winter, lilac-pink flowers. *B.* 'Wintermärchen' has dark green leaves that are tinged with red in winter, red flowers.

WINTER APPEAL Large, glossy evergreen leaves tinged with red and purple

PERIOD OF WINTER INTEREST Throughout.

VALUE FOR REST OF THE YEAR Valuable ground cover all year round; white, pink or deep red flowers in spring.

SIZE Most varieties will reach about 30-45 x 30-45cm (12-18 x 12-18in) in three years.

CULTIVATION NOTES

Moderately hardy, tolerating -10 to -15°C (14 to 5°F), although some forms may suffer damage to foliage or

Epimedium

   ❝ *I have grown epimediums almost as long as I have gardened and they now occupy some of the more inhospitable bits of my present garden where they elicit admiration from the many visitors who don't know them. They are relatively tolerant both of shade and dryness but they have an added value that isn't always appreciated: the foliage generally persists until well into the winter. A few species, of which* E. rubrum *is much the best, have fine autumn colour that persists too.* ❞

WINTER APPEAL Persisting, delicate, sometimes red-tinged foliage.

PERIOD OF WINTER INTEREST Autumn to late winter.

VALUE FOR REST OF THE YEAR Foliage changes colour through the seasons; red, white or yellow flowers in spring.

SIZE Most forms will reach about 30-45 x 30-45cm (12-18 x 12-18in) after three years; although classed as ground cover, they shouldn't be considered invasive and some are merely clump forming.

CULTIVATION NOTES

Moderately hardy, tolerating -10 to -15°C (14 to 5°F); best in light to medium shade, but tolerates deep shade; best in rich, moist soil, but tolerates fairly dry soil too; cut back dead foliage in spring. Propagate by division in spring or autumn.

Recommended varieties

Epimedium peralderianum has more or less oval, bronze-green leaves that later become glossy and deep green, bright yellow flowers in spring. *E. pinnatum* has glossy, rounded, bright green leaves, bright yellow flowers in early summer. *E. x rubrum* is a creeping, ground-covering plant with heart-shaped leaves that are green and red when young, turning red-brown in autumn, crimson and yellow flowers in late spring.

Epimedium pinnatum colchicum

Euphorbia

❝ *Euphorbias have been popular garden plants for many years. But nothing matches the sales they have achieved in recent years as an increasing range of species and varieties have become available. There may be a lack of variety in the flowers (although that could be said of many other groups) but there is a wide range of overall shapes and forms that means there is a place in most spots in most gardens that a Euphorbia could fill. Two varieties have proved extremely useful in my winter borders.* ❞

WINTER APPEAL Evergreen or semi-evergreen foliage, sometimes red-purple in winter.
PERIOD OF WINTER INTEREST Throughout.
VALUE FOR REST OF THE YEAR Green-yellow flowerheads from spring to early summer.
SIZE Varies, but the recommended varieties will reach about 75 x 50cm (30 x 20in) after three years.

CULTIVATION NOTES

The recommended forms are moderately hardy, tolerating -10 to -15 °C (14 to 4°F) although the foliage will be browned rather unattractively in cold wind; *E. amygdaloides* 'Purpurea' prefers light shade, but *E. a.* 'Robbiae' is best in medium to deep shade; moist, humus-rich soil. Propagate by seed, basal cuttings in spring, semi-ripe cuttings in late summer by removal of offsets, suckers or by division (you will appreciate that *E. a.* 'Robbiae' is a very easy plant to multiply and can be invasive).

Recommended varieties

E. amygdaloides 'Purpurea' has green leaves tinged with red-purple, and cup-shaped bright yellow flowerheads in spring; *robbiae* has larger, dark green leaves and lime-green flowerheads in spring.

Euphorbia amygdaloides 'Robbiae'

Helleborus Hellebore

> ❝ *The winter in my garden would be a much drearier time was it not for the hellebores. This is despite the fact that the most reliable winter-blooming form,* H. foetidus, *has green flowers, but they are of a delicate green and contrast as effectively with the much darker shade of the foliage as if they were bright yellow. Hellebores are among the few really good, really reliable evergreen herbaceous perennials although you must realise that 'evergreen' is a relative term. The old leaves must be cut back in late winter.* ❞

WINTER APPEAL Purple, pink, cream or green flowers; attractive palmate foliage often retained through the winter, even in deciduous species.

PERIOD OF WINTER INTEREST Late winter to early spring, depending on species.

VALUE FOR REST OF THE YEAR Constant foliage interest and, in some species, flowers that persist until well into the spring.

SIZE About 30-60 x 30-45cm (12-24 x 12-18in) after three years.

CULTIVATION NOTES

Most forms are hardy, tolerating -20°C (-4°F) but the delicate flowers of *Helleborus niger* are always best when given protection by cloche from the winter rain; best in light to medium shade, with some shelter, ideally in a woodland situation or shrubbery; tolerates most soils, but best in a moist, organic loam that is more or less neutral; to tidy up the plants, remove dead or damaged leaves in spring by cutting them back to soil level. Propagate by basal, rooted cuttings in spring, or the species by seed.

Helleborus niger

Recommended varieties

H. argutifolius has pale green flowers and dark green leaves that last through winter. *H. atrorubens* has deep purple flowers that open before the dark green purple-tinged leaves, and purple stems. *H. foetidus* has very long-lasting green flowers, sometimes fragrant, sometimes edged with purple, and dark green leaves that give off an unpleasant smell when crushed, this is the best winter-flowering hellebore; 'Wester Fisk', green flowers, grey-green leaves and red stems. *H. lividus* has cream flowers tinged with green and purple, glossy blue-green leaves that last through winter and purple stems. *H. niger* (Christmas rose) has pink-white flowers with green centres, leathery dark green leaves that last through winter and purple stems, but despite its name, it doesn't reliably flower at Christmas and different strains open their flowers over several weeks; 'Potter's Wheel', larger, white flowers with green centres. *H. x nigercors* has white or pink flowers and mid-green leaves that last through winter. *H. orientalis* (Lenten rose) has white, green or cream flowers and deep green leaves that last through winter. This is a very variable species and one of the delights of gardening is to wait for the flowers of the self sown seedlings. *H. purpurascens* has purple-pink to grey flowers that open before the leathery mid-green leaves. *H. x sternii* has cream-green flowers tinged with purple, mid-green leaves that last through winter, and purple stems. *H. torquatus* has purple flowers that open before the mid-green leaves. *H. viridis* has green flowers that open before the dark green leaves.

Hepatica

66 *Many gardeners wax lyrical over* Anemone blanda *and its allies; and so, to a degree, do I. But I also pay tribute and give garden space to their close relatives, the hepaticas. In that, I differ from a good many of my fellows. For* Hepatica *is one of the unsung heroes of early spring, its delicate, delightful flowers being too little appreciated and seen. Perhaps I can correct an injustice.* 99

Hepatica nobilis

WINTER APPEAL Anemone-like blue, pink or white flowers.
PERIOD OF WINTER INTEREST Early spring.
VALUE FOR REST OF THE YEAR Mid-green, kidney-shaped leaves.
SIZE Slow-growing, reaching only 10-15 x 15-20cm (4-6 x 6-8in) after three years.

CULTIVATION NOTES
Moderately hardy, tolerating -10 to -15°C (14 to 5°F); best in partial shade, in a rich, moist, well-drained, neutral to alkaline soil, but will tolerate heavier soils. Propagate by division in spring, or by seed.

Recommended varieties
H. acutiloba has blue, pink or white flowers. *H. x media* 'Ballardii' has semi-double deep blue flowers. *H. nobilis* has blue, pink or white flowers, often on bare stems. *H. transsilvanica* has blue or white flowers and semi-evergreen leaves.

Heuchera Coral Flower

66 *Heucheras are well worth growing for their delicate summer flowers and they aren't generally bought for their value in winter. But once established in the garden, the all-year-round merit of the glossy leaves becomes very apparent.* 99

WINTER APPEAL Evergreen or semi-evergreen foliage in shades of purple and green.
PERIOD OF WINTER INTEREST Throughout.
VALUE FOR REST OF THE YEAR Delicate inflorescences of pink, red or white summer flowers.
SIZE 30-45 x 30-60cm 12-18 x 12-24in) after three years.

CULTIVATION NOTES
Most forms are moderately hardy, tolerating -10 to -15°C (14 to 5°F); best in full sun or partial shade, in a rich, moist, well-drained neutral soil. Propagate species by seed, species or varieties by division in autumn.

Recommended varieties
H. 'Palace Purple' has large, heart-shaped metallic-purple leaves and cream flowers with red anthers, followed by pink seed heads. *H.* 'Pewter Moon' has similar leaves and large pink flowers. *H. sanguinea* has kidney-shaped pale and dark green marbled leaves and large red, pink or white flowers; many other varieties have leaves similar to those of *H. sanguinea,* with flowers in a range of bright reds, pinks and even green.

Heuchera 'Snowstorm'

Liriope

❝ *Not many people grow* Liriope *for its flowers. In truth, not many people grow* Liriope *for any decorative purpose, regarding it more as a utilitarian plant. For, undeniably, it makes a very good evergreen ground cover in warm, dry places. It's sometimes called lily turf, a reference to its sward forming capabilities. It does make a valuable foil for other things but I should add that if you are thinking of a mixed planting with bulbs, be aware that they will have their work cut out to compete with a* Liriope *turf just as much as they would with one of real grass.* ❞

WINTER APPEAL Evergreen strap-shaped leaves, sometimes variegated.
PERIOD OF WINTER INTEREST Foliage throughout; some forms flower throughout the autumn; black autumn fruits.
VALUE FOR REST OF THE YEAR Dense purple flower spikes in summer or autumn. In mild seasons, they may persist into winter.
SIZE 20-30 x 30-45cm (8-12 x 12-18in) after three years.

CULTIVATION NOTES
Hardy, tolerating -15 to -20°C (5 to -4°F); best in partial or deep shade with shelter from cold winds; light, rich, moist, well-drained soil, preferably acidic. Propagate by seed or by division in spring.

Recommended varieties
L. exiliflora 'Ariaka-janshige' (syn. 'Silvery Sunproof') has green leaves striped with white and gold, and pale purple flowers in late summer. *L. muscari* has dark green leaves and bright mauve flowers in autumn; 'John Burch', gold-variegated leaves and larger flowers.

Liriope muscari

Ophiopogon

❝ Ophiopogon *has become a relatively familiar plant; and a very striking one too. However, gardeners, even experienced ones, make two very common mistakes about it. First, they think it a grass which most assuredly it isn't, being a member of the lily family (and, coincidentally, very closely related to* Liriope*). And second, they think that it has black leaves. It doesn't, nothing does. But some varieties of* Ophiopogon *have the darkest leaves of any plant I know and, although in reality a very deep purple, they are certainly striking if you use them in the right place. But there is absolutely no point in growing* O. planiscapus *'Nigrescens' unless it is set off against something light and fresh. Otherwise, in the short, dark days of winter, you just won't see it.* ❞

WINTER APPEAL Evergreen grass-like foliage in attractive and unusual colours, sometimes variegated.
PERIOD OF WINTER INTEREST Throughout.
VALUE FOR REST OF THE YEAR Pink, white or lilac flowers in summer followed by glossy blue or black fruits.
SIZE *O. jaburan* will reach about 60 x 30cm (24 x 12in) after three years, *O. planiscapus* about half this height.

Ophiopogon planiscapus 'Nigrescens'

Pachysandra

❝ I've never really felt that Pachysandra *lives up fully to expectations; at least in my garden. So by what token does it become a 'best winter plant'? The answer is that I have seen it growing so well and so effectively in other places that I simply conclude that my garden conditions aren't exactly right (or that I'm a poor gardener, which is much harder to accept). I think that a slightly heavy soil is the key to success. Then it will form a most appealing lush green carpet through which other, more dramatic things will grow to great effect. ❞*

WINTER APPEAL Glossy evergreen ground-cover foliage.
PERIOD OF WINTER INTEREST Throughout.
VALUE FOR REST OF THE YEAR Small white flowers in spring or early summer.
SIZE 15-25 x 60cm (6-10 x 24in).

CULTIVATION NOTES
O. jaburan is hardy, tolerating about -15°C (5°F), but *O. planiscapus* is very hardy tolerating -15 to -20°C (5 to -4°F); full sun or partial shade; often said to be best in slightly acidic soil although it grows well enough in neutral conditions in my garden; moisture, good drainage and fertility are more important. Propagate by seed, or division in spring.

Recommended varieties
O. jaburan 'Vittatus' has pale green leaves that are edged and striped with cream, yellow or white. *O. planiscapus* 'Nigrescens' has extremely dark purple-black leaves, slightly paler and more green at the base.

CULTIVATION NOTES
Hardy, tolerating -15 to -20°C (5 to -4°F); full or partial shade; any except very dry soil. Propagate by division in spring, or softwood cuttings in early summer.

Recommended varieties
P. terminalis 'Green Carpet' has small, glossy, finely-toothed dark green leaves, and small white flowers; 'Variegata' has white-edged leaves and can look very appealing but it is very much slower growing and scarcely deserving of the name 'ground cover'.

Pachysandra terminalis 'Variegata'

Petasites

❝ When I was a child, we lived close to a small river whose banks were clothed with a very strongly smelling plant that we called wild rhubarb. It was Petasites hybridus, *a very large, odd and invasive plant with rather few redeeming features, beyond serving as a jungle for small boys' games. It's a native riverside species but it has a much smaller, although also rather invasive, Mediterranean relative that has been grown in gardens for some 200 years. This is the plant that I commend. The winter heliotrope has that rather special appeal that attaches to plants whose flowers appear on naked stems before the leaves emerge. ❞*

WINTER APPEAL Sweetly fragrant flowers of unusual and curious form that appear shortly before the leaves.
PERIOD OF WINTER INTEREST Mid-winter to early spring.
VALUE FOR REST OF THE YEAR Large, rounded leaves making useful ground cover.
SIZE 30cm x 1.5m (12in x 5ft) after three years.

CULTIVATION NOTES
Hardy, tolerating 15 to -20°C (5 to -4°F); partial or full shade (good hedge bottom plant); deep, organic soil: *P. fragrans* tolerates drier conditions than others. Divide in spring or autumn.

Recommended varieties
P. fragrans (Winter heliotrope) has vanilla-scented white or pale lilac flowers and dark green leaves.

Petasites fragrans

Phormium New Zealand Flax

❝ There's a good deal of mischief talked about phormiums. On countless occasions, I've seen them described as tender; and the variegated varieties too tender even to be tried in most temperate gardens. This is arrant nonsense. The plain green forms are pretty tough and even some of the striped types have come through hard winters in my own rather cold garden with minimal protection. Certainly, the more variegation and the more colour in the leaves, the less hardy they are, but within sensible limits, they will survive in a good many places.

And to what end? Because there are few plants that have the size, sword-like leaves and overall stature to make such a statement in the garden, in winter or summer.

The name 'New Zealand Flax' alludes to the long-standing use of the plant's leaf fibres to make rope and twine. It has been grown commercially for this purpose in many parts of the world although today, it's as an ornamental that Phormium *is better known. ❞*

Phormium tenax

WINTER APPEAL Striking ever-green foliage in various colours, sometimes variegated.
PERIOD OF WINTER INTEREST Throughout.
VALUE FOR REST OF THE YEAR The clumps of sword-shaped leaves provide constant interest, useful as a focal point; tall inflorescences in summer.
SIZE 2-4 m x 2-3 m (6$^1/_2$-13 x 6$^1/_2$-10ft).

CULTIVATION NOTES

Varies with variety from barely hardy, tolerating 0 to -5°C (32 to 23°F) to moderately hardy, tolerating -10 to -15°C (14 to 5°F): in areas prone to hard frost, mulch heavily in winter; best in full sun; fertile, moist, well-drained soil. Propagate by division in spring.

Recommended varieties
Phormium cookianum hookeri 'Cream Delight' has light green leaves striped and edged with creamy yellow; 'Tricolor' has light green leaves edged with yellow and red; the 'Maori' series includes several hybrids and selections of *P. cookianum* with leaves striped in various shades of apricot, pink, red and bronze. P. 'Sundowner' has bronze-green leaves edged with dark pink, and panicles of yellow-green flowers. *P. tenax* 'Purpureum' has red-purple leaves and red flowers. P. 'Yellow Wave' has yellow-green leaves striped with darker green, and red flowers.

Physalis Chinese Lantern

❝ *Hectares of this plant must be grown commercially for the dried flower arranging trade. And understandably so, for there is nothing else quite like it in its striking colour and form; and its ability to retain both when dried. In truth, it's probably better dried than left in the winter garden where those brightly coloured fruits tend to discolour and decay. If you do want to leave it in the garden, therefore, try to ensure that it's grown in a warm but sheltered spot.* ❞

WINTER APPEAL Brightly-coloured long-lasting calyces containing the fruits.
PERIOD OF WINTER INTEREST Autumn to early spring.
VALUE FOR REST OF THE YEAR Mid-green foliage; small summer flowers.
SIZE 60-75 x 90cm (24-30 x 34in) after three years, and spreads vigorously.

Physalis alekengi franchetii

CULTIVATION NOTES

Moderately hardy, tolerating -10 to -15°C (14 to 5°F); full sun or very light shade; any well-drained soil. May be propagated by division in spring although I find it's always best when grown afresh from seed.

Recommended varieties
Physalis alkekengi franchetii, a form of Chinese lantern, has bright orange-red fruits contained in expanded papery red calyces, and small cream flowers in summer.

Pulmonaria
Lungwort

❝ *I know that winter is approaching its end when from my kitchen window, I first see the yellow clump of primroses contrasting with the faint blue haze of a surrounding carpet of pulmonaria flowers, some 30 metres (100 yards) away across the lawn. In cold years, admittedly, the pulmonaria is hidden until well into spring but it is consistently one of the earliest of herbaceous perennials in mine and most other people's gardens.* ❞

WINTER APPEAL White, blue or red flowers; semi-evergreen foliage, sometimes attractively mottled or variegated.
PERIOD OF WINTER INTEREST Late winter to mid-spring.
VALUE FOR REST OF THE YEAR Foliage interest and useful ground cover often throughout the year and certainly until well into the summer.
SIZE About 25-35 x 45cm (10-14 x 18in) after three years, though *P. rubra* is more vigorous and may spread to twice this size.

CULTIVATION NOTES
Hardy, tolerating -15°C (5°F) or below; best in light to medium shade, but *P. officinalis* will tolerate full sun; best in a moist but well-drained, deep, rich, fertile loam, not good in dry places; remove shrivelled leaves in autumn. Propagate by division in spring or autumn.

Recommended varieties
P. angustifolia has deep blue flowers, sometimes tinged with pink, and mid-green leaves; 'Munstead Blue', bright blue flowers, small dark green leaves. *P.* 'Lewis Palmer' has pink flowers that later turn bright blue, and dark green leaves spotted with white. *P.* 'Mawson's Blue' has dark blue flowers and dark green leaves, a wonderful variety, probably the best blue but not easy to find. *P. officinalis* 'Sissinghurst White' has white flowers that open from pink buds, and white-spotted leaves. *P. rubra* has bright red flowers (which never look quite right to me; I like my pulmonarias blue) and bright green leaves; 'David Ward', bright red flowers and grey-green leaves with cream edges.

Pulmonaria officinalis

Sedum

❝ Sedum *is a very big genus and one that is amply represented in the rock garden where it can certainly add winter appeal (page 88). But there are a few herbaceous sedums that have an equally valuable role in the herbaceous border. Their rather striking flowerheads attract the second-generation red admirals and small tortoiseshells from miles around and they go on to become bedecked, not with insects, but with the crystals of winter frost.* ❞

WINTER APPEAL Flowerheads remain attractive through autumn, and are popular in dried flower arrangements.
PERIOD OF WINTER INTEREST Autumn to early winter.
VALUE FOR REST OF THE YEAR Glaucous or fleshy foliage; flowers first appear in summer.
SIZE 45-60 x 45-60cm (18-24 x 18-24in) after three years.

CULTIVATION NOTES

Moderately hardy, tolerating -10 to -15°C (14 to 5°F); best in full sun to light shade; neutral to alkaline, well-drained, fairly fertile soil; divide every three or four years to encourage flowering. Propagate by seed in spring or division in spring.

Recommended varieties

S. 'Herbstfreude' (syn. 'Autumn Joy') bears flat flowerheads that turn from green to pink, bronze and coppery-red, and glaucous light green leaves. S. spectabile (Ice plant) bears pink flowerheads, and grey-green leaves; 'Brilliant' has brighter pink flowers.

Sedum 'Herbstfreude'

Yucca

❝ *There's not much else really like* Yucca. *Phormiums are rather similar in form but their leaves are softer and more pliable. Yuccas have the thrusting, aggressive spikes that have become such an integral part of the twentieth century architectural garden. Yet they do look oddly out of place in the older informality of a cottage environment. Even in appropriate surroundings, however, choose them carefully and plant them carefully; the first because many are tender, and the second because those leaf tips are truly vicious and should never be placed where someone may catch an eye as they pass.* ❞

WINTER APPEAL Dramatic, erect, sword-shaped leaves, sometimes variegated.
PERIOD OF WINTER INTEREST Throughout.
VALUE FOR REST OF THE YEAR Foliage provides constant 'architectural' feature; panicles of white flowers in mid- to late summer.
SIZE Y. filamentosa will reach about 75cm x 1.5m (30in x 5ft) after three years, Y. gloriosa about 2 x 2m (6½ x 6½ft).

CULTIVATION NOTES

Y. filamentosa (Adam's needle) is very hardy, tolerating -15 to -20°C (5 to -4°F). Y. gloriosa is moderately hardy, tolerating around -10°C (14°F), and in colder areas will need to be wrapped in hessian or similar material during the winter; best in full sun with shelter from cold winds; well-drained, fairly rich soil, tolerant of some alkalinity; remove outer dead leaves in autumn. Propagate by division in spring, root cuttings in winter or, best of all, by removal of offsets in spring.

Recommended varieties

Y. filamentosa 'Bright Edge' has dark green leaves with gold margins; 'Variegata', blue-green leaves edged with white that take on a pink tinge in winter. Y. gloriosa 'Variegata' has dark green leaves edged with yellow, and purple-tinged flowers.

Yucca gloriosa 'Variegata'

Ferns

" *My garden, any garden, would be a less interesting place without ferns. Yes, they lack flowers and fruits but they display such a wide range of leaf size and shape that they can never bore you. A great many ferns are deciduous, with nothing to show in the winter, but a great many aren't; the very fact that fern specialists tend to call them 'winter green' rather than evergreen serves to emphasise their value. In many respects indeed, it is when flowers are so sparse in the cold months, that the evergreen fern really comes into its own. But do not ignore the deciduous ferns, because some retain their foliage well into the winter, some have appealing autumn colours and those that begin growth in early spring can contribute the fascination of the unfurling young fronds.* "

Adiantum Maidenhair Fern

WINTER APPEAL Semi-evergreen foliage; brightly coloured new shoots.
PERIOD OF WINTER INTEREST Late winter to early spring.
VALUE FOR REST OF THE YEAR Constant foliage interest.
SIZE *Adiantum pedatum* will reach about 30-40 x 30-40cm (12-16 x 12-16in), *A. venustum* will grow about 15cm (6in) high and spread vigorously.

CULTIVATION NOTES
Very hardy, tolerating -20°C (-4°F); best in light to deep shade; moist, organic, fairly rich soil. Propagate by division in early spring.

Recommended varieties
A. pedatum is semi-evergreen with long narrow mid-green fronds with glossy dark brown stems. *A. venustum* is evergreen or semi-evergreen with triangular mid-green fronds with black stalks, and bright pink new fronds that appear in late winter to early spring.

Asplenium trichomanes

Asplenium

WINTER APPEAL Bright, glossy evergreen foliage.
PERIOD OF WINTER INTEREST Throughout.
VALUE FOR REST OF THE YEAR Constant foliage interest.
SIZE Most reach about 45-70 x 60-80cm (18-28 x 24-32in); A. s. 'Undulatum' will reach only about 30 x 50cm (12 x 20in).

CULTIVATION NOTES
Very hardy, tolerating -20°C (-4°F) or below; partial shade; moist, well-drained, organic soil, preferably with added grit; propagate by division in spring.

Recommended varieties
Asplenium scolopendrium (Hart's tongue fern) is hugely variable but typically has tongue-shaped, glossy bright green fronds with wavy edges; 'Cristatum' has crests at the tips of the fronds; 'Kaye's Lacerated', 'frayed' margins; 'Undulatum', fronds with very wavy edges.

Blechnum Hard Fern

WINTER APPEAL Leathery evergreen foliage.
PERIOD OF WINTER INTEREST Throughout.
VALUE FOR REST OF THE YEAR Constant foliage interest.
SIZE *Blechnum penna-marina* will reach about 10-20cm (4-8in) in height and spread vigorously but very prettily; *B. spicant* about 20-50 x 60cm (8-20 x 24in) or more; *B. tabulare* 1 x 1m (3 x 3ft).

CULTIVATION NOTES
B. penna-marina and *B. spicant* are very hardy, tolerating -20°C (-4°F). *B. tabulare* is fairly hardy, tolerating -10°C (14°F); best in humid conditions in partial or deep shade; moist, organic, acid soil. Propagate by spores in summer or division in spring. See Book 3, *Best Shade Plants*, for information on raising from spores.

Recommended varieties

B. penna-marina has narrow, glossy, pinnate fronds that are reddish when they first appear. *B. spicant* has narrow, leathery, mid-green pinnate evergreen sterile fronds that lie flat on the ground in a rosette formation, and deciduous fertile ones, which look like a fish skeleton, standing erect. *B. tabulare* has lance-shaped mid-green sterile fronds and fringed brown fertile fronds.

Polypodium

WINTER APPEAL Delicate evergreen foliage.
PERIOD OF WINTER INTEREST Throughout.
VALUE FOR REST OF THE YEAR Constant foliage interest; excellent ground-cover.
SIZE *P. vulgare* 'Cornubiense' will grow about 30-40cm (12-16in) high and spread very vigorously.

CULTIVATION NOTES

Very hardy, tolerating -20°C (-4°F) or below; full sun or dappled shade, with shelter from cold winds; best in well-drained, fairly fertile, organic, gritty soil but tolerant both of high alkalinity and dryness. Propagate by division in spring or early summer.

Recommended varieties

P. v. 'Cornubiense' is much the best form and has dense, lobed fronds that grow darker with age; it makes excellent ground cover.

Polypodium vulgare

Polystichum
Shield Fern

WINTER APPEAL Dense, prickly foliage, usually evergreen, with fronds often rather tightly curled.
PERIOD OF WINTER INTEREST Throughout.
VALUE FOR REST OF THE YEAR Constant foliage interest.
SIZE 60-90 cm x 40-90cm (24-34 x 16-34in) after three years.

CULTIVATION NOTES

Very hardy, tolerating -20°C (-4°F); partial or deep shade; organic, well-drained soil. Can be surprisingly tolerant of dryness. Propagate by division in spring.

Recommended varieties

Polystichum aculeatum has glossy, leathery, dark green fronds with prickly lobes. *P. polyblepharum* has glossy dark green fronds, at first covered in golden hairs, lobes with toothed edges. *P. setiferum*, the best species, has dark green fronds and toothed lobes; 'Acutilobum' Group, sharp bristles on fronds; 'Congestum' Group, fronds tightly curled and often crested; 'Divisilobum' Group has fronds divided into narrow leathery segments; 'Divisilobum Densum', overlapping feathery fronds; 'Perserratum' Group, upright habit with finely toothed edges to fronds. *P. tsussimense* has dark green markedly upright fronds.

GRASSES

Grasses

" *The value of ornamental grasses has been one of the gardening discoveries of recent years. Perhaps, this is because they blend with many of the modern garden features: gravel, architectural plants and minimal maintenance. The range in leaf colour available is huge, from golds to the closest that any leaf comes to real blue.* "

Calamagrostis Reed Grass

WINTER APPEAL Striking, long-lasting inflorescences in interesting colours.
PERIOD OF WINTER INTEREST Throughout.
VALUE FOR REST OF THE YEAR Flowers first appear in midsummer; arching, glossy leaves form an 'architectural' feature.
SIZE 1.8m x 60cm (6ft x 24in) after three years.

CULTIVATION NOTES
Hardy, tolerating -15 to -20°C (5 to -4°F); sun or partial shade; moist, organic soil but will tolerate most; cut back to soil level in early spring. Propagate by division in mid-spring.

Recommended varieties
Calamagrostis acutiflora 'Karl Foerster' has pinkish-bronze inflorescences that later turn light brown; 'Overdam', yellow-edged and striped leaves, turning pink-white.

Deschampsia Hair Grass

WINTER APPEAL Long-lasting flower spikelets in various colours; tussocks of dense, evergreen leaves.
PERIOD OF WINTER INTEREST Throughout.
VALUE FOR REST OF THE YEAR Flowers first appear in early summer; constant foliage interest.
SIZE *Deschampsia cespitosa* will reach about 2 x 1.2-1.5m (6 1/2 x 4-5ft) after three years; *D. flexuosa* only 60 x 30cm (24 x 12in).

CULTIVATION NOTES
Hardy, tolerating -15 to -20°C (5 to -4°F); sun or partial shade; best in a moist, neutral to acid soil; remove dead flowerheads in early spring. Propagate by seed in spring or autumn, or division in spring or early summer.

Recommended varieties
D. cespitosa 'Bronzschleier' (syn. 'Bronze Veil') has rigid, rough, linear leaves and arching panicles of silver-bronze flowerheads; 'Goldschleier' (syn. 'Gold Veil'), dark green leaves and silver-yellow flowerheads; 'Goldtau' (syn. 'Gold Dew'), red-brown flowerheads that later turn golden. *D. flexuosa* 'Tatra Gold' has arching yellow-green leaves and bronze flowerheads.

Deschampsia cespitosa 'Golden Veil'

Festuca Fescue

WINTER APPEAL Dense tufts of blue-green leaves, usually evergreen.

PERIOD OF WINTER INTEREST Throughout.

VALUE FOR REST OF THE YEAR Spikelets of green, orange, yellow or violet flowers in late spring to late summer.

SIZE Most forms reach 30-50 x 15-25cm (12-20 x 6-10in) after three years.

CULTIVATION NOTES

Hardy, tolerating -15 to -20°C (5 to -4°F); best in full sun; poor to fairly fertile, dry, well-drained soil; divide every two or three years to ensure strong leaf colour. Propagate by seed in autumn or spring, or division in spring.

Festuca glauca

Recommended varieties

Festuca amethystina has grey-green leaves and purple-green flowers. *F. glauca* 'Blaufuchs' (syn. 'Blue Fox') has blue leaves and blue-green flowers; 'Blauglut' (syn. 'Blue Glow'), intense silver-blue leaves. *F. valesiaca* has blue-green leaves and violet-green flowers; 'Silbersee' (syn. 'Silver Sea'), silver-blue leaves.

Hakonechloa

WINTER APPEAL Beautifully variegated bright yellow-green leaves tinged with red.

PERIOD OF WINTER INTEREST Autumn to early winter.

VALUE FOR REST OF THE YEAR Constant foliage interest; flowers in late summer and autumn.

SIZE 35 x 40cm (14 x 16in) after three years.

CULTIVATION NOTES

Hardy, tolerating -15 to -20°C (5 to -4°F); full sun or partial shade; rich, moist, well-drained soil; propagate by division in spring.

Hakonechloa macra 'Aureola'

Recommended varieties

The best and commonest form *Hakonechloa macra* 'Aureola' has yellow leaves striped with green that take on a red tinge in autumn, and pale green flower spikelets in summer and autumn; a superb grass.

Luzula Rush

WINTER APPEAL Colourful evergreen foliage, sometimes variegated.

PERIOD OF GREATEST WINTER INTEREST Throughout.

VALUE FOR REST OF THE YEAR Constant foliage interest and useful ground cover; small flowers in spring and summer.

SIZE 70-80 x 45cm (28-32 x 18in) after three years.

CULTIVATION NOTES

Moderately hardy, tolerating -10 to -15°C (14 to 5°F); best in partial or deep shade; fairly fertile, organic, moist but well-drained soil. Propagate by seed in spring or autumn, or division in late spring or early summer.

Recommended varieties

Luzula sylvatica 'Aurea' has broad shiny yellow-green leaves that turn bright yellow in winter, and small red-brown flowers; 'Marginata', mid-green leaves edged with cream, and pendent brown and yellow flowers.

GRASSES

Carex Sedge

WINTER APPEAL Graceful, arching evergreen foliage, often variegated.

PERIOD OF WINTER INTEREST Throughout.

VALUE FOR REST OF THE YEAR Constant foliage interest; flowers from late spring to late summer.

SIZE Ranges from 10 x 10cm (4 x 4in) after three years for *C. firma* 'Variegata' to 1 x 1m (3 x 3ft) or more for *C. flagellifera* and *C. pendula*, with the other recommended forms between these.

CULTIVATION NOTES

Most are hardy to very hardy, tolerating -20°C (-4°F), but *C. morrowii* 'Fisher's Form' is only moderately hardy, tolerating around -10°C (14°F); sun or partial shade; fertile, at least fairly moist soil suits most; remove dead leaves in summer. Propagate by division in late spring or early summer.

Carex hachijoensis 'Evergold'

Recommended varieties

C. firma 'Variegata' has stiff, glossy blue-green leaves edged with yellow, and small dark brown flower spikes. *C. flagellifera* has broad green or red brown leaves, light brown flower spikes, red-brown fruit. *C. hachijoensis* 'Evergold' has dark green leaves with a yellow central stripe, brown flower spikes. *C. morrowii* 'Fisher's Form' has broad, glossy mid-green leaves with cream stripes and edges, green and brown flower spikes. *C. pendula* has broad, glossy mid-green leaves, blue-green on the underside, cylindrical brown flower spikes, erect at first, pendent when mature. *C. siderosticha* 'Variegata' has broad, pale green leaves with white stripes and edges, tinged with pink at the base, and light brown flower spikes.

Cortaderia Pampas Grass

WINTER APPEAL Tall, striking, long-lasting plumes of flowers and narrow evergreen foliage.

PERIOD OF WINTER INTEREST Autumn to early winter.

VALUE FOR REST OF THE YEAR Flowers first appear in early summer; constant foliage interest.

SIZE Most will attain 2.5-3 x 1.5-2.5m (8-10 x 5-8ft) after three years and are therefore too tall for many gardens where 'Pumila', which is about half this size, is a much better choice for the majority of gardeners.

Cortaderia selloana 'Sunningdale Silver'

CULTIVATION NOTES

Cortaderia selloana is very hardy, tolerating -20°C (-4°F), but C. *richardii* is moderately hardy, tolerating -10 to -15°C (14 to 5°F); protect young crowns in first winter; best in full sun, in a spacious site; fertile, well-drained soil; pull out old flowering stems and dead leaves with strong gloves (don't set fire to plants) in late winter or early spring. Propagate by division in spring.

Recommended varieties

C. richardii has leathery, olive-green leaves and creamy-white or silvery flower plumes. *C. selloana* has glaucous, mid-green leaves and silvery-pink or purple flowers; 'Aureolineata', gold-edged leaves; 'Pumila', lower growing, mid-green leaves and silvery-yellow flowers; 'Sunningdale Silver', particularly tall, tough, flower stems bearing silvery-white plumes.

Miscanthus

WINTER APPEAL Long-lasting, silky flower panicles in delicate shades.
PERIOD OF WINTER INTEREST Late autumn to early winter.
VALUE FOR REST OF THE YEAR Flowers first appear in late summer; arching, linear leaves, often blue-green, with silvery mid-ribs.
SIZE Most forms will reach 1-2 x 1.5-2m (3-6$\frac{1}{2}$ x 5-6$\frac{1}{2}$ft) after three years, but be warned, M. *sinensis* may reach 4m (13ft) in height.

CULTIVATION NOTES

M. sacchariflorus is moderately hardy, tolerating -10 to -15°C (14 to 5°F), but the other forms are very hardy, tolerating -20°C (-4°F); best in full sun; prefers a fairly fertile, moist, well-drained soil, but tolerates most; cut back the previous year's flower stems in early spring. Propagate by seed in spring, or division in spring.

Recommended varieties

M. floridulus has pale green leaves with silver mid-ribs and silvery flower spikelets. *M. sacchariflorus* has erect blue-green leaves with silvery mid-ribs and silky silvery-white flower spikelets. *M. sinensis* has blue-green leaves and silky purple-grey flower spikelets; 'Gracillimus', narrow leaves with white mid-ribs that turn bronze in autumn; 'Silberfeder' (syn. 'Silver Feather'), excellent for its profuse flowering, its silvery-pinkish-brown panicles reliably persisting through winter; 'Zebrinus', mid-green leaves with most unusual and dramatic cream or yellow horizontal stripes.

Miscanthus sinensis

Stipa Hair Grass

WINTER APPEAL Feathery flower panicles, valuable for dried arrangements; often evergreen foliage that may change colour.
PERIOD OF WINTER INTEREST Autumn to early winter.
VALUE FOR REST OF THE YEAR Flowers first appear in early or mid-summer; constant foliage interest.
SIZE *Stipa arundinacea* will reach about 1 x 1.2m (3 x 4ft) after three years, S. *gigantea* about twice this size and S. *tenuissima* about half.

CULTIVATION NOTES

Hardy to very hardy, tolerating -15°C (5°F) or below; best in full sun, though S. *arundinacea* tolerates partial shade; prefers a fairly fertile, light to medium, well-drained soil; cut back deciduous species in early winter, and remove dead leaves from evergreens in early spring. Propagate by seed in spring, or division in late spring to early summer.

Recommended varieties

S. arundinacea has evergreen, inrolled, rather tough dark green leaves with orange-brown streaks in summer turning almost completely orange-brown in winter, and pendent purple-green flower panicles. S. *gigantea* has evergreen or semi-evergreen, inrolled, mid-green leaves and bristly, purple-green, oat-like flower spikelets later turning gold. S. *tenuissima* is deciduous with very narrow, inrolled, bright green leaves, feathery, green-white flower panicles.

Agapanthus African Lily

" *A summary of* Agapanthus *that I wrote some years ago reads, 'A beautiful summer-flowering South African bulb for warm gardens'. So it may seem surprising that it now finds its way into my book on winter plants. I would still only recommend it for milder gardens but, in such places, I have found the evergreen forms still lush and green in winter and providing a splendid foil to other plants through the grey winter days so I couldn't, in fairness, do other than include it.* "

WINTER APPEAL Clumps of strap-shaped, arching dark green leaves, sometimes evergreen.

PERIOD OF WINTER INTEREST Evergreen forms throughout, deciduous ones autumn to early winter.

VALUE FOR REST OF THE YEAR Magnificent heads of blue or white trumpet-shaped flowers in summer, followed by attractive seedheads.

SIZE About 90cm-1m x 50cm (34in-3ft x 20in) after five years, and eventually spreading much more.

CULTIVATION NOTES

The narrow-leaved and deciduous forms are moderately hardy, tolerating -10 to -15°C (14 to 5°F), but the broad-leaved evergreen forms are barely hardy, tolerating 0 to -5°C (32 to 23°F); protect crowns with mulch in winter; best in full sun with shelter from cold winds, and thrives especially well in mild coastal gardens; prefers a moist, well-drained, rich, organic soil, and is intolerant of poor or water-logged conditions; cut off dead flower spikes after flowering. Propagate by seed, or division in spring.

Recommended varieties
A. *africanus* is evergreen with deep blue-purple flowers, white in albus. A. *campanulatus* is deciduous; patens is the best form, a smaller, plant with flowers pale to mid-blue; the 'Headbourne Hybrids' are the best for summer flowering and can be very attractive when frosted in the winter.

Amaryllis

" *Amaryllis is generally promoted as a late summer- or autumn-flowering bulb but I have seen it in sheltered gardens in full bloom in early winter. It is the time of the first frost that really limits its ambitions and, as the first frosts are tending to occur later, I include it for mild gardens.* "

WINTER APPEAL Splendid, fragrant heads of funnel-shaped flowers in white, pink and purple.

PERIOD OF WINTER INTEREST Autumn to early winter.

VALUE FOR REST OF THE YEAR Visible only during flowering season.

SIZE Up to 60cm (24in) in height, spreading to about 30cm (12in) after five years.

CULTIVATION NOTES

Moderately hardy, tolerating around -10 °C (14°F), and foliage should be protected from frost; full sun or very light shade, with shelter from cold winds; light but fairly fertile, well-drained soil. Propagate by division.

Agapanthus 'Headbourne Hybrids'

Amaryllis belladonna

Recommended varieties
Amaryllis belladonna (Jersey lily) bears pink, funnel-shaped flowers on purple stems, followed by fleshy mid-green leaves. There are several varieties with white or purple flowers too and a few are always available but those offered vary from supplier to supplier.

Anemone
Wind Flower

" *Few things in my garden give more joy than the appearance of the first, small, bulbous anemones, pushing their blue, white or pink flowers through the soil at a time when a dusting of snow is as likely as not to fall and decorate them. They are so easy to grow and take up so little room in nooks and corners that it almost seems cruel not to plant them. And although they are the gems of the end of winter, I've included here for convenience their non-bulbous relative* A. x hybrida *which brings cheer at the other end of the season, its clear flowers on tall stems lasting well beyond autumn.* "

WINTER APPEAL Pretty blue, white or pink flowers.
PERIOD OF WINTER INTEREST
Most of the recommended bulbous varieties flower in spring, but *A. x hybrida* flowers in autumn.
VALUE FOR REST OF THE YEAR
Conspicuous only during flowering season.
SIZE The spring-flowering forms that I recommend here are small, about 10-20cm (4-8in) in height, spreading to about 20-45cm (8-18in) after five years, *A. ranunculoides* being the lowest and most spreading; the autumn-flowering *A. x hybrida* may grow as tall as 1m (3ft) in one season and spread slowly but indefinitely.

CULTIVATION NOTES
Very hardy, tolerating -20°C (-4°F); all of my recommended varieties are best in full sun or light shade; moist, fairly rich but free-draining soil. Propagate by seed, or division: autumn-flowering varieties in spring or autumn, rhizomatous/tuberous varieties such as *A. apennina* and *A. blanda* in late spring.

Recommended varieties
A. appennina usually has blue flowers, sometimes white or pinkish-white, and dark green palmate leaves. *A. blanda* has deep blue, white or pink flowers, and dark green palmate leaves; 'Ingramii', deep blue flowers with purple undersides; 'White Splendour', large white flowers with pinkish undersides. *A. x hybrida* (Japanese anemone) blooms in late summer to mid-autumn: the variety 'Geante des Blanches' has semi-double white flowers with greenish undersides and palmate mid-green leaves; 'Honorine Jobert', much the finest form, single white flowers with pinkish undersides and yellow stamens. *A. ranunculoides* has buttercup-yellow flowers and lobed, mid-green leaves.

Anemone blanda

Chionodoxa Glory of the Snow

“ *There's an area of my gravel garden that simply bursts into flower in the late winter when the masses of self-sown chionodoxas come into bloom. They are one of the under-valued glories of the early season; but do be a tiny bit careful of that self-seeding as they can get everywhere.* ”

WINTER APPEAL Dainty star-shaped flowers.
PERIOD OF WINTER INTEREST Late winter to early spring.
VALUE FOR REST OF THE YEAR Visible only during flowering season.
SIZE About 10 x 5cm (4 x 2in) after two years.

CULTIVATION NOTES

Hardy, tolerating -15°C (5°F); full sun to light or moderate shade; light, free-draining soil, slightly acid to slightly alkaline. Propagate by removal of self-sown seedlings or afresh from seed.

Recommended varieties

Chionodoxa luciliae has bright blue flowers with white centres and mid-green, arching leaves.

Chionodoxa luciliae

Crocus

“ *A crocus flower for every month is just about possible. So consider them as more than merely colour to accompany the early daffodils. Choose carefully and give them protection from the worst winter rain, and one crocus or another will bring you joy for weeks.* ”

WINTER APPEAL Purple, white or yellow-orange flowers.
PERIOD OF WINTER INTEREST Autumn to spring, depending on variety.
VALUE FOR REST OF THE YEAR Visible only during flowering season.
SIZE Most of the recommended forms will reach a height of 5-10cm (2-4in) and spread to 5cm (2in) after two years, but *Crocus speciosus* may reach a height of 15cm (6in).

CULTIVATION NOTES

Very hardy, tolerating -20°C (-4°F); full sun to light shade; thrives in most soils except very heavy or very waterlogged, and tolerates some alkalinity and acidity; pull away shrivelled foliage, and if grown in grass, do not mow until six weeks after flowering. Propagate by seed or division, but leave plants undisturbed for as long as possible.

Recommended varieties

C. ancyrensis has bright yellow or orange, late winter and early spring. *C. banaticus*, large lilac or purple, early autumn. *C. etruscus* 'Zwanenburg' lilac-blue, late winter to spring. *C. imperati* 'De Jager', violet-purple, brownish with violet stripes on the outside, late winter to early spring, and shiny dark green leaves. *C. korolkowii*, fragrant bright yellow, late winter to early spring. *C. kotschyanus*, pale lilac with yellow-dotted throats and cream stamens, autumn. *C. laevigatus* 'Fontenayi', lilac-purple, mid-winter. *C. longiflorus*, fragrant, light to dark lilac with orange styles, autumn, and white-striped leaves. *C. medius* bright or pale purple with orange styles, late autumn. *C. ochroleucus*, cream-white with yellow throats, late autumn. *C. sativus*, purple-veined, lilac with deep red styles that produce saffron, autumn. *C. sieberi* 'Albus', white with dark yellow throats, early spring; 'Hubert Edelsten', pale lilac, deep purple outers with white stripes, late winter to early spring; *sublimis* 'Tricolor', lilac-, white- and yellow-striped, late winter to early spring. *C. speciosus*, violet-blue with dark blue veins and orange styles, autumn; 'Albus', pure white, autumn. *C. tommasinianus*, lilac to red-purple with silver outer parts, late winter to spring; 'Whitewell Purple', red-purple, silver-mauve inside, late winter to spring. *C. tournefortii*, pale lilac with orange styles and white anthers, late autumn to winter.

Crocus tommasinianus

Cyclamen

❝ *Cyclamen are the mainstay of ground-covering interest in many a garden through the winter, either through their flowers or their beautifully shaped and patterned leaves. You quite simply cannot be without them but do remember to mulch them with leaf mould during the summer to encourage seeds to germinate and the colony to spread.* ❞

WINTER APPEAL Delicate, sometimes fragrant, flowers in white, pink or red; attractive heart-shaped, patterned leaves appear from autumn onwards.
PERIOD OF WINTER INTEREST Autumn to spring, depending on variety.
VALUE FOR REST OF THE YEAR Visible only during flowering season.
SIZE Most will reach about 10 x 10cm (4 x 4in) after two or three years.

CULTIVATION NOTES

Cyclamen coum and *C. hederifolium* are very hardy, tolerating -20°C (-4°F) or below; *C. libanoticum* is barely hardy and is really best in a cool greenhouse; *C. cilicium, C. mirabile* and *C. pseudoibericum* are fairly hardy, tolerating -5 to -10°C (23 to 14°F); full sun to moderate shade; best in a moist, organic soil, but will tolerate thin soil beneath deciduous trees if given organic mulch. Propagate by seeds or division. Cyclamen self seed very readily.

Cyclamen coum

Recommended varieties
C. hederifolium has pink flowers, sometimes fragrant, with maroon mouths, in mid- to late autumn, and beautiful triangular or heart-shaped, patterned, mid- to dark green leaves, sometimes purple underneath; appears in many more or less distinct varieties with variously patterned leaves; *album*, pure white flowers. *C. coum* has white, pink or red flowers with dark red mouths, in winter or early spring, and rounded dark green or silver-patterned leaves; it appears in many more or less distinct varieties with variously patterned leaves; *album*, white flowers with dark red mouths. *C. cilicium* has white or pink flowers with deep red mouths in autumn, and heart-shaped mid-green leaves with darker shading. *C. libanoticum* has pale or mid-pink flowers, white at the base, with deep red mouths, from winter to early spring, and heart-shaped, dull green leaves patterned with lighter green. *C. mirabile* has pale pink flowers with maroon mouths in autumn, and heart-shaped mid-green leaves with scalloped edges, purple-red underneath. *C. pseudoibericum* has fragrant magenta flowers with darker mouths in winter to spring, and heart-shaped dark green leaves marked with silver-grey.

BULBS

Eranthis Winter Aconite

❝ *The buttercup has some wonderful and immediately identifiable relatives. But none is more welcome nor more splendid than the aconites, with their vivid little golden-yellow bowls. They sit on a mound of attractively dissected foliage that expands as they fade, to form itself a pleasing and very pretty ground cover for a few more weeks.* ❞

WINTER APPEAL Bright yellow buttercup-like flowers.
PERIOD OF WINTER INTEREST Late winter to early spring.
VALUE FOR REST OF THE YEAR Attractive foliage for several weeks in the spring.
SIZE Grows to about 10cm (4in) high and will spread to about 10cm (4in) after two years.

CULTIVATION NOTES
Hardy, tolerating -15°C (5°F); best in light to moderate shade, but will tolerate full sun; best in organic, woodland soil but will tolerate most. Propagate by seed (in many gardens they self-sow with ease) or division in spring. But be aware that they can be difficult to establish in some gardens.

Recommended varieties
Eranthis hyemalis is the most popular form, with bright yellow flowers and dissected, bright green leaves; *tubergenii* 'Guinea Gold', similar flowers that appear slightly earlier, and bronze-green leaves.

Eranthis hyemalis

Erythronium Dog's Tooth Violet

❝ *Dog's tooth violets are often not very obvious. But that has less to do with the flowers themselves than where they grow, for they are essentially plants of damp and shaded places. They need to be sought out, but what better reward for a little persistence in the garden in the cold early of days of spring than to chance on such a splendid surprise.* ❞

Erythronium dens-canis

WINTER APPEAL Dainty pink, purple, white or yellow curled-back flowers.
PERIOD OF WINTER INTEREST Late winter to early spring.
VALUE FOR REST OF THE YEAR Visible only during flowering season.
SIZE Most will reach about 20-25 x 10-15cm (8-10 x 4-6in) after two years.

CULTIVATION NOTES

Moderately hardy, tolerating -10 to -15°C (14 to 5°F); light to moderate shade; prefers a moist, rich, organic, slightly acidic soil. Propagate by division after flowering.

Recommended varieties

Erythronium californicum 'White Beauty' has creamy-white flowers with a red ring around the base, and dark green brown-mottled leaves. *E. dens-canis* has white, pink or lilac flowers with purple or blue anthers, and mid-green leaves marbled with purple-brown. *E.* 'Pagoda' has bright yellow flowers with brown rings at the centre, and glossy dark green bronze-mottled leaves. *E. tuolumnense* has clusters of bright yellow flowers with green veins and pale or mid-green leaves.

Galanthus Snowdrop

❝ *Botanists define one of the most loved groups of all plants with the bald statement, 'Galanthus, a genus of about 12 species in the Family Liliaceae (Section Amaryllidaceae) occurring from Western Europe to Iran'. I know that the season is very much in their favour and I've often said that if snowdrops occurred in summer, they wouldn't receive nearly as much attention. But they don't occur in summer, they brighten up the dull weeks of mid-winter and if one plant could be said to epitomise that well-worn phrase, 'harbinger of Spring', Galanthus is it.* ❞

Galanthus nivalis

WINTER APPEAL Welcome white flowers, sometimes fragrant.
PERIOD OF WINTER INTEREST Most forms flower from mid-winter to early spring, but some, such as *G. caucasicus,* may start to flower in the autumn.
VALUE FOR REST OF THE YEAR Visible only during flowering season.
SIZE Most forms reach about 10-15 x 8-10cm (4-6 x 31/2-4in) after four years, but there are some smaller varieties and some very striking tall ones, such as *G.* 'Atkinsii' and *G.* 'S. Arnott', that may reach 35m (14in) in height and spread to 10cm (4in) in two years.

CULTIVATION NOTES

Most are very hardy, tolerating -20°C (-4°F); best in light to medium or even deep shade, though they will tolerate full sun; best in moist, well-drained, fairly rich organic soil, but tolerates most; pull away shrivelled foliage at least six weeks after flowers have faded. Propagate by seed, or division after flowering.

Recommended varieties

Snowdrop varieties always sound more distinct in description than they look in reality: 'yellow' and 'green' are relative terms in flower colour as they are all predominately white. A distinguishing feature is often the size and shape of the marks at the tip of the flower's inner parts or tepals. *G. allenii* has almond-scented flowers with large green marks. *G.* 'Atkinsii', long flowers with heart-shaped green marks on superb long stalks. *G. caucasicus* may flower as early as late autumn; its flowers have single green marks. *G. elwesii,* honey-scented flowers with two green markings on each inner tepal. *G. ikariae ikariae,* large green marks. *G.* 'Lady Beatrix Stanley', double flowers with tiny green marks. *G.* 'Magnet', large, long-stalked flowers, with inverted V-shaped green marks. *G. nivalis* (Common snowdrop) small flowers with inverted V-shaped marks; 'Flore Pleno', irregularly double flowers; 'Lady Elphinstone', double flowers with yellow markings; 'Pusey Green Tip', irregularly double flowers with pale green markings on the outer tepals; 'Viridapicis', a very long spathe, or bract, and green marks on the outer tepals. *G. plicatus* has single green marks, and wide, dull green leaves with curved edges; *byzantinus,* green marks at the base and apex of each tepal. *G.* 'S. Arnott', large, honey-scented flowers with inverted V-shaped marks, probably the tallest of all snowdrops.

Ipheion

66 *If there is a prize for the bulb with the longest lasting appeal,* Ipheion *must be a strong candidate for it. Its very pretty leaves appear long before the flowers; and the flowers then continue, at first a few but later more, for week after week. And it is simplicity itself to grow.* 99

WINTER APPEAL Clumps of strap-shaped, usually blue-green, leaves.
PERIOD OF WINTER INTEREST Throughout.
VALUE FOR REST OF THE YEAR Fragrant, star-shaped flowers appear in spring.
SIZE 10-20cm x 10-15cm (4-8 x 4-6in) after three years.

Ipheion uniflorum

CULTIVATION NOTES
Very hardy, tolerating -20°C (-4°F), but may be damaged by long periods of frost and should be mulched in winter in colder places; best in full sun; fairly fertile, organic, moist but well-drained soil. Propagate by seed, or by division or removal of off-sets in summer.

Recommended varieties
Ipheion uniflorum has honey-scented silver-blue flowers and light blue-green leaves that smell of onions when crushed; the superb form *I. u.* 'Froyle Mill', violet flowers; *I. u.* 'Wisley Blue', lilac-blue flowers.

Iris

66 *There are few pleasures in winter gardening to match the discovery of the winter-flowering iris. Those characteristically beautiful lipped flowers are so much associated with spring and then with the heat of summer, that their presence in winter is a joyous revelation. But plant them in your warmest soil and then leave them undisturbed.* 99

Iris unguicularis

WINTER APPEAL Large, fragrant flowers and evergreen foliage.
PERIOD OF WINTER INTEREST Late winter to early spring.
VALUE FOR REST OF THE YEAR Rather little; there is constant foliage interest although this can become rather untidy in summer.
SIZE 30 x 15cm (12 x 6in) after three years.

CULTIVATION NOTES
Moderately hardy, tolerating -10 to -15°C (14 to 5°F); full sun and needs the warmest spot in your garden, ideally the base of a warm wall; very well-drained, neutral to alkaline soil. Propagate by seed, division or offsets.

Recommended varieties
Iris unguicularis (still sometimes called *I. stylosa*) bears pale or deep purple flowers with yellow markings, sometimes as early as late autumn; 'Mary Barnard' has violet flowers in mid-winter.

Leucojum
Snowflake

66 *Leucojums are essentially giant and magnificent snowdrops, yet many fewer gardeners know and love them. But do choose the right species: just remember that the autumn snowflake flowers in autumn, the summer snowflake flowers in spring and the one for present purposes, the spring snowflake, flowers in winter.* 99

WINTER APPEAL White flowers that first begin to appear around the time the snowdrops fade.

PERIOD OF WINTER INTEREST Early spring.

VALUE FOR REST OF THE YEAR Invisible except during flowering season.

SIZE 20-30 x 8cm (8-12 x 31/2in) after three years.

CULTIVATION NOTES

Hardy, tolerating -15 to -20°C (5 to -4 °F); light to moderate shade; best in moist, free-draining, rich soil but tolerates most conditions including moderate acidity and alkalinity; propagate by seed or offsets.

Recommended varieties

Leucojum vernum has bell-shaped white flowers with green tips, and shiny dark green strap-shaped leaves.

Leucojum vernum

Narcissus

❝ *What is a winter flowering narcissus in some places will be a proper spring variety in others. Nonetheless, I've selected those that brighten up at the least the latter part of winter in my own garden in the centre of England and is about half-way between extremes.* ❞

WINTER APPEAL Splendid yellow or white flowers in many shades, sometimes fragrant.

PERIOD OF WINTER INTEREST Late winter and early spring.

VALUE FOR REST OF THE YEAR None, and the dying foliage can become rather untidy.

SIZE Most forms grow to 15-30cm (6-12in) high and spread to about 20cm (8in) after three years.

Recommended varieties

Narcissus asturiensis is dwarf, with pale yellow flowers in late winter and early spring. *N. bulbocodium* has golden-yellow flowers in mid-spring; conspicuus is the best form. *N.* 'Cragford', fragrant white flowers with bright orange perianth segments, early spring. *N. cyclamineus,* pendent golden flowers with upswept petals, late winter to early spring. *N.* 'Dove Wings', small white perianth segments with pale yellow trumpets, mid-spring. *N.* 'February Gold', golden perianth segments with darker trumpets, early spring. *N.* 'Grand Soleil d'Or', fragrant, double gold and orange flowers, late autumn to early spring but a plant for

CULTIVATION NOTES

With few exceptions, very hardy, tolerating -20°C (-4°F); full sun to light shade, and tolerant of strong winds; tolerates most soils, including moderate alkalinity and acidity; do not cut back until at least six weeks after flowers have faded, and do not tie leaves in knots; propagate by division of large clumps; and always plant bulbs with their base around 15cm (6in) deep.

Narcissus 'February Gold'

mild areas. *N.* 'Little Gem', dwarf, with golden-yellow flowers, early spring. *N. minor*, dwarf with bright yellow flowers, early spring. *N. obvallaris,* small, golden flowers, early spring. *N.* x *odorus*, fragrant golden flowers, early spring. *N. pseudonarcissus,* twisted yellow perianth segments with golden trumpets, early spring. *N. romieuxii*, small with variable flowers that may be straw- or primrose-coloured, early spring. *N. tazetta,* many fragrant flowers on each stem: their colours vary, and there are many 'bunch-flowered' varieties related to it. *N.* 'Tête-à-Tête', dwarf, bearing golden perianth segments with deeper yellow trumpets, early spring.

BEDDING PLANTS

The very name Bedding Plant conjures up an image of the summer; of pricking on seedlings and transferring them to the cold frame in order to have strong plants to put out as the danger of frost recedes. They are all annuals, either genuine annuals or half-hardy perennials that will not survive the winter in our climate and are therefore grown as annuals. Clearly such plants have no part to play in the winter garden. Nonetheless, winter bedding plants do exist. Some are small hardy perennials, some biennials. They are few in kind but large in value and in recent years, one group in particular, the winter flowering pansies, has become hugely important.

Viola Pansy

6 6 *The development of new and improved varieties of winter flowering pansy has been, I think, one of the unsung gardening revolutions of recent years. They have left behind all other pretenders to the title of winter bedding. In containers or in beds (and provided a little care and thought is given to their cultivation), I have no hesitation in guaranteeing that they will provide attractive and reliable flowers right through the winter, whatever the weather. And to be able to say that about what appear superficially to be flimsy little perennials is a remarkable state of affairs.* 9 9

WINTER APPEAL Large, typical pansy flowers in a range of strong, bold colours, including white, blues, purples and mauves and oranges with some bicolours and some of the familiar pansy 'face' patterns.
PERIOD OF WINTER INTEREST Throughout.
VALUE FOR REST OF THE YEAR Flowering will continue through the spring and into early summer although I think it a mistake to try to keep them going for too long (aphids begin to take a serious interest as the temperature rises) and they should then be replaced by proper summer bedding.
SIZE Well cared for, plants should attain about 20 or 25 cm in height.

CULTIVATION NOTES
Moderately Hardy, tolerating around -10 to -15°C (14 to 4°F); the plants will be bowed low by snow and frost but will rise again. They must however be placed in the sunniest spot available. But whether you raise your own from seed or buy them in the autumn, it's essential that you obtain the biggest, strongest specimens possible; and they must have flower buds at the time of planting. Many gardeners express disappointment that their winter pansies have failed to bloom and this is almost invariably because the plants were not sufficiently mature in the autumn. Do remember that it's very difficult indeed to persuade a plant that is merely a rosette of leaves to begin flower initiation as the temperature falls. The cost of large plants may be double that of small ones, but it is worth paying.

Winter-flowering pansies

Recommended Varieties

All winter flowering pansies belong to the same complex hybrid group *Viola x wittrockiana* as the summer flowering types. The main groups of winter and early spring flowering types are the 'Universal' and 'Ultima' series and I have found these to be the most reliable although you will see others including the Jewel, Forerunner, Imperial and Regal ranges. Different nurseries, garden centres and seed companies offer their own preferred range and different colours within each.

'Universal' pansies

'Universal' pansies in a hanging basket

Other Winter Bedding Plants

Although the winter flowering pansy is the winter bedding plant supreme, others can play a supporting role. For the later part of the winter, some of the brightly coloured 'primroses' of the *Primula* x *pruhoniciana* types are effective (page 86). Their main drawback however is that many of them are just too bright (some of the pinks are almost luminous) and they do need placing with great care. Some frankly clash with everything else that isn't green. The outer leaves soon discolour unattractively in cold wet weather moreover and must be tidied away regularly.

In mild seasons, wallflowers (*Cheiranthus cheiri*) will be in flower by late winter although their real merit comes in the spring. The drawback to having wallflowers in the winter garden (especially in containers or in a small garden) however is that they take up a great deal of room while offering only green leaves. And in severe winters, they can be rendered both unattractive and useless. Among other plants that are useful in combination with pansies in winter containers, including hanging baskets, are small evergreen shrubs such as conifers, thymes or *Euonymus,* climbers/trailers such as ivies and vincas and foliage plants like ajugas, *Tolmeia, Cineraria maritima*, and the dead nettles, especially the yellow flowered *Lamium galeobdolon*. Details of these can be found in Book 8, *Best Container Plants*.

ALPINES

Dianthus Pink

   " *Dianthus are almost totally unappreciated for their contribution to winter garden appeal; and I admit they were unappreciated by me until I looked closely at a small bed close to my kitchen door. In admiring the bright colours of the crocuses, cyclamen and other early season bulbs, I only then realised that their effect was enhanced the more for pushing through the grey-blue of dianthus leaves* "

WINTER APPEAL Attractive evergreen linear or lance-shaped foliage, often blue-grey.
PERIOD OF WINTER INTEREST Throughout.
VALUE FOR REST OF THE YEAR Profuse, long-lasting, often fragrant flowers borne throughout the early summer.
SIZE 5-15 x 10-20 cm after three years.

CULTIVATION NOTES
Moderately hardy, tolerating -10 to -15°C (14 to 4°F); needs full sun or very light shade; light, free-draining, neutral to highly alkaline soil: intolerant of acidity; remove dead flower heads with shears after flowering; propagate by shoot tip or basal cuttings in late summer, by layering, or some forms by seed. Plants deteriorate fairly quickly and will probably need replacing after four years.

Recommended Varieties
D. alpinus, glossy, dark green foliage and deep pink, toothed flowers spotted with paler pink; *D. myrtinervius,* tiny, with bright green leaves and single, deep pink flowers with pale centres; *D. petraeus,* mid-green leaves and single, fragrant, toothed white flowers; *D. subacaulis,* dark green leaves and single deep pink flowers.

Dianthus alpinus 'Joan's Blood'

Primula Primrose

   " *Primroses are among the best loved spring flowers; but I've never known why they are so seldom recognised for their value in flowering in sheltered spots well before winter is through. And this is true of many of their relatives too in this immensely beautiful if sometimes challenging genus. Nor are primulas in general as widely appreciated as they should be for the attractiveness of their leaves which can be among the prettiest in the winter garden* "

Primula denticulata alba

Primula vulgaris

WINTER APPEAL Bright and cheerful flowers, but, in a few varieties, with extraordinarily garish colours that are impossible to blend with anything. Some later spring flowering types nonetheless have particularly attractive foliage.

PERIOD OF WINTER INTEREST Late winter to early spring.

VALUE FOR REST OF THE YEAR Some have more or less evergreen foliage.

SIZE Most of those that I recommend will reach about 7-15 x 15-25 cm after three years, though *P. elatior* may reach twice and *P. denticulata* three times this size.

CULTIVATION NOTES

Moderately hardy, tolerating -10 to -15°C (14 to 4°F); *P. allionii* needs full sun or partial shade and a gritty, alkaline soil; *P. berninae, P. denticulata, P. elatior; P. farinosa, P. frondosa, P. juliae* and *P. vulgaris* need full sun or partial shade and a fertile, organic, moist but well-drained neutral to acid soil; *P. nana, P. petiolaris, P. x scapeosa* and *P. sonchifolia* need partial or deep shade, and a peaty, gritty, moist but very well-drained acid soil; propagate by seed, or by division immediately after flowering. Division every three or four years is essential with many varieties to maintain vigour. And this is most of all true of the double forms of *P. vulgaris*.

Recommended Varieties

P. allionii, many varieties, bearing white, pink or purple flowers with white eyes, late winter to spring, evergreen, grey-green leaves; *P. x berninae,* purple flowers in spring and deciduous mid-green leaves; *P. denticulata,* 'drumstick' heads of white, lilac or purple flowers in spring; *P. elatior,* Oxlip, heads of tubular yellow flowers in spring and summer, evergreen or semi-evergreen mid-green leaves; *P. farinosa,* heads of lilac-pink flowers with yellow eyes, in late spring and early summer, deciduous mid-green leaves; *P. frondosa,* lilac to red-purple flowers with yellow eyes in late spring and early summer, deciduous mid-green leaves; *P. juliae,* magenta flowers with yellow eyes in spring and summer, semi-evergreen dark green leaves; *P. nana,* (syn. *edgeworthii*), heads of white, pink, lilac or blue flowers with yellow and white eyes in late winter to spring, deciduous pale green leaves; *P. petiolaris,* purple flowers with yellow eyes and narrow white edges in spring, evergreen mid-green leaves; *P. x scapeosa,* pink-purple flowers in spring, more or less evergreen, mid-green leaves; *P. sonchifolia,* heads of lavender-blue flowers with yellow eyes and white edges in spring, deciduous mid-green leaves; *P. vulgaris,* Common primrose, pale yellow, often fragrant, flowers from early to late spring, evergreen or semi-evergreen bright green leaves; many early-flowering and brightly coloured hybrids between *P. vulgaris* and *P. juliae* are available.

ALPINES

Saxifraga Saxifrage

❝ *Saxifrages are arguably the most important plants in the alpine garden, summer or winter. But they are a huge and confusing group and whilst I feel that only one sub-group of the genus is of real winter merit (see below), you may not find it easy to locate all of my selections. The ideal is to visit one of the several large and excellent alpine plant nurseries in winter and simply select the plants that offer the greatest appeal at the time you see them* ❞

WINTER APPEAL There are several different groups of Saxifrage, each with a distinctive form of foliage. Only one group, Porophyllum, flowers very early in the year, and forms rosettes of usually evergreen, lime-encrusted leaves.
PERIOD OF WINTER INTEREST Throughout.
VALUE FOR REST OF THE YEAR Constant foliage interest.
SIZE Most of the forms that I recommend here reach about 10 x 15 cm after three years.

CULTIVATION NOTES
Moderately hardy, tolerating -10 to -15°C (14 to 4°F); the encrusted forms recommended need full sun, and a very well-drained, alkaline soil, ideally in pockets between limestone rocks; carefully pull away dead leaves; propagate by offsets in early spring, or some forms by seed.

Recommended Varieties
'Arco', pale lilac flowers and mid-green leaves; 'Bodensee', pink-yellow flowers, mid-green leaves; S. *burseriana*, cup-shaped white flowers and grey-green leaves; 'Edith', pink flowers, silver-grey leaves; 'Eulenspiegel', bright yellow flowers, mid-green leaves; S. *ferdinandi-coburgi*, cup-shaped, bright yellow flowers and light grey leaves; S. *frederici-augusti grisebachii*, red-purple flowers, grey-green limy leaves; S. x *gloriana*; 'Gregor Mendel', pale yellow flowers, green leaves; 'Iris Pritchard', pale pink or salmon flowers, silver-green leaves; 'Johann Kellerer', lilac-salmon flowers, silver-greed leaves; 'King Lear', white flowers, grey-green leaves; 'Kolbiana', pale yellow flowers, mid-green leaves; S. *lilacina*, deep violet veined flowers, grey-green leaves S. *marginata*, panicles of white or pink-flushed flowers and silvery-grey leaves; 'Robin Hood' deep pink flowers, mid-green leaves; 'Rosemarie', rose-pink flowers, mid-green leaves; S. *sancta*, cup-shaped green-yellow flowers with conspicuous anthers, and bright green leaves; S. *sempervivum*, cup-shaped white flowers on red stems, and blue-green leaves; 'Sofia', yellow flowers, blue-green leaves; S. *stolitzkae*, white flowers, grey, limy leaves.

Saxifraga 'Gregor Mendel'

Sedum Stonecrop

❝ *As well as the larger Sedums for the herbaceous border (see page 68), there are many smaller, mat-forming varieties for rock gardens. Often they have attractive ever-green foliage in various shades, sometimes glaucous, sometimes forming rosettes. They are very pretty but can be insidiously invasive and rapidly subjugate a small-rock garden.* ❞

WINTER APPEAL Distinctive, succulent evergreen foliage forming a ground covering mat in various shades of green and mauve.
PERIOD OF WINTER INTEREST Throughout.
VALUE FOR REST OF THE YEAR Tiny, usually star-shaped flowers in summer.
SIZE Most rock-garden forms reach a height of 5-10 cm and spread to 40-60 cm after three years.

Sedum spathulifolium

CULTIVATION NOTES

Hardy to Very hardy, tolerating around -20°C (-4°F); best in full sun or very light shade; thrives in most well-drained soils, tolerating acidity and alkalinity; propagate by offsets, division or softwood cuttings in spring, or some forms by seed. Many types are very fragile stemmed and fragment to form readily rooting pieces and so may become invasive.

Recommended Varieties

As with many alpine plants, your choice will be dictated by what is available but among the prettiest and most readily obtainable are: *S. kamtschaticum* 'Variegatum', semi-evergreen, mid-green leaves with cream edges, tinged with pink, yellow flowers turning red; *S. spathulifolium,* rosettes of spoon-shaped silvery-green leaves tinged with purple-bronze, bright yellow flowers, the commonest form is the striking 'Cape Blanco'; *S. spurium,* mid-green leaves, red stems, pinkish-purple or white flowers.

Sempervivum Houseleek

❝ *I know why sepervivums should be associated with houses as they commonly grow on old roofs in moist regions. But why anyone should imagine they look like leeks is much less clear. Their distinctive spiny rosettes have a very special appeal and a trough or other container planting of them can look utterly delightful with a dusting of winter snow.* ❞

WINTER APPEAL Distinctive succulent evergreen rosettes of thick, pointed, often bristly or hairy leaves, commonly tinged with purple or red and sometimes festooned with cobweb-like fibres.
PERIOD OF WINTER INTEREST Throughout.
VALUE FOR REST OF THE YEAR Star-shaped white, yellow, red or purple flowers on relatively tall stems in summer.
SIZE Very slow-growing: most will reach 10-15 x 15-30 cm after eight years.

CULTIVATION NOTES

Moderately hardy to Hardy, tolerating around -10 to -15°C (14 to 4°F); full sun to very light shade; very well-drained, gritty soil; remove dead rosettes; propagate by offsets, or some forms by seed.

Sempervivum montanum

Recommended Varieties

Sempervivum is another large alpine plant genus with, in many instances, relatively little difference between the species and consequent difficulties with identification. The following are distinctive winter plants among the more widely available types but look also at the closely related genus *Jovibarba* which differs in flowers but has similar winter foliage appeal: *Sempervivum arachnoideum,* variable leaves but always with cobweb fibres, tomentosum is the best form, pink-red flowers; *S. marmoreum* 'Ornatum', vivid red leaves with green tips, white flowers; *S. tectorum,* blue-green leaves with purple tips, deep pink flowers;

Clematis

" Other than the odd bloom during mild spells or in abnormally early or late seasons, no clematis flowers in the winter. But I couldn't leave the late-flowering species out of any account of winter plants for the quite special beauty of their seedheads. At their best, they are light, silvery and feathery; at worst, a little dishevelled and brown. But with frost and winter dew on them, they have inspired countless artists and photographers for very obvious reason. And this is justification alone for not pruning clematis until early spring, as I have always advocated. "

Clematis orientalis 'Bill Mackenzie'

WINTER APPEAL Attractive feathery seedheads, sometimes semi-evergreen foliage.

PERIOD OF WINTER INTEREST Autumn to early winter.

VALUE FOR REST OF THE YEAR Prolific flowers in summer, sometimes fragrant.

SIZE The more vigorous forms, such as *Clematis akebioides, C. flammula, C. potaninii, C. rehderiana, and C. tangutica* will grow 3-4m (10-13ft) each year, even with hard pruning, and if unpruned will reach 5-6m (16-20ft) eventually; the less vigorous forms, such as *C. aethusifolia, C. texensis* and *C. viorna,* will reach 1-2m (3-6½ft) after one year and with annual pruning will reach 2-3m (6½-10ft) each year.

CULTIVATION NOTES

The varieties recommended here are generally moderately hardy, tolerating -10 to -15°C (14 to 5°F), except *C. orientalis, C. rehderiana, C. tangutica* and *C. texensis,* which are hardy to very hardy tolerating around -15 to -20°C (5 to -4°F); tolerant of all aspects; the more vigorous forms are best scrambling through trees, the less vigorous are suitable for training against walls; tolerates most soils, but always does best in moderately alkaline, deep, rich loam; prune late-flowering species in early spring, cutting back all of the previous season's growth to a pair of strong buds about 75cm (30in) above soil level. Propagate by seed, softwood cuttings in early summer, or by layers.

Recommended varieties
Seedheads are all more or less silver-white and feathery; flower details are for late summer or autumn: *C. aethusifolia* has bell-shaped, pale yellow flowers, delicate, fern-like leaves. *C. akebioides* has masses of small yellow or green-yellow flowers, darker on the outside. *C. armandii* is the only hardy evergreen species with elongated leathery leaves and richly scented white flowers in early spring. *C. flammula* is semi-evergreen with masses of almond-scented single white flowers. *C. orientalis* has lantern-shaped green-yellow flowers. *C. potaninii* has relatively few, silky white flowers. *C. rehderiana* has clusters of fragrant, tubular, pale yellow flowers. *C. tangutica* has masses of bell-shaped golden-yellow flowers. *C. texensis* has bell-shaped bright red flowers. *C. tibetana* has green-yellow to orange flowers. *C. viorna* has jug-shaped orange-brown or red-purple flowers with cream tips. *C. vitalba* is vigorous but wonderful in the wild garden.

Lonicera Honeysuckle

" Like clematis, honeysuckles don't flower in winter; but unlike them they do not have seedheads. What some species offer instead is the appeal of a scrambling mass of stems, evergreen leaves and/or persisting fruits; although birds generally find the latter before they can fully be appreciated. "

CULTIVATION NOTES

Most of the recommended varieties are moderately hardy, tolerating -10 to -15°C (14 to 5°F); tolerates full sun to moderate shade, and best grown through trees; prefers a moist, organic loam and dislikes very wet or very dry conditions; pruning not essential, but one third of the oldest shoots may be cut back to soil level each spring to improve vigour. Propagate by semi-ripe cuttings in summer, or layers.

WINTER APPEAL The forms included here have evergreen or semi-evergreen foliage, and some-times autumn berries.
PERIOD OF WINTER INTEREST Throughout.
VALUE FOR REST OF THE YEAR Often fragrant flowers in summer.
SIZE Most forms included here will reach about 2 x 2m (6 1/2 x 6 1/2ft) after five years and 6-10m (20-33m) after 20 years.

Recommended varieties

(All evergreen or semi-evergreen)
L. alseuosmoides has cream flowers with purple tint in late summer, vivid blue fruits. *L. henryii* has dark green leaves, paler underneath, red-purple flowers in summer to autumn; black berries. *L. implexa* has cream-yellow flowers through the summer. *L. japonica* 'Halliana' has bright green leaves, fragrant white summer flowers that turn pale yellow; 'Aureoreticulata', bright green leaves with yellow veins, white flowers turning yellow. *L. splendida* has blue-grey leaves, cream and pink summer flowers, orange fruits.

Hydrangea

« The deciduous climbing hydrangea has become a popular plant, mainly for its appealing, open white flowerheads during the summer. But as their plants grow older, many gardeners come to appreciate that it has another quite different appeal in winter when the coloured, flaking bark develops. And a few fortunate gardeners in milder places will soon realise the value of its much less well known evergreen relative. »

WINTER APPEAL Evergreen foliage in some forms, autumn colour in others.
PERIOD OF WINTER INTEREST Autumn or throughout.
VALUE FOR REST OF THE YEAR Showy summer flowers.
CULTIVATION NOTES
H. petiolaris is hardy, tolerating -10 to -15°C (14 to 5°F), but *H. serratifolia* is barely hardy, tolerating 0 to -5°C (32 to 23°F); full sun to moderate shade: *H. petiolaris* thrives against a shady wall; best in a rich, moist, well-drained soil, tolerating acidity and alkalinity; pruning not necessary; propagate by layering.
SIZE 2 x 2m (6 1/2 x 6 1/2ft) after five years, 12-14 x 12-14 (40-46 x 40-46ft) eventually.

Recommended varieties

H. petiolaris has deciduous dark green, ovate to rounded leaves that turn yellow in autumn, white fertile and sterile flowers in summer. *H. serratifolia* has evergreen, leathery, dark green leaves, and clusters of white flowerheads in summer.

Lonicera fragrantissima

Hydrangea petiolaris

CLIMBERS

Celastrus Bittersweet, Staff Vine

❝ Celastrus *isn't evergreen and nor does it have winter flowers. Its fruits and their seeds, however, can match the display that any winter plant can offer. But do be warned; you really must have both male and female plants, for the sexes are separate; there are so-called hermaphrodite strains but I must be unfortunate for I have never had one that produces anything.* ❞

Celastris orbiculatus

WINTER APPEAL Colourful autumn fruits and seeds, if male and female plants are grown together; autumn foliage colour.
PERIOD OF WINTER INTEREST Autumn to early winter.
VALUE FOR REST OF THE YEAR Small flowers in summer.
SIZE May reach a height of 14m (46ft) eventually, and needs sturdy support.

CULTIVATION NOTES
Moderately hardy, tolerating -10 to -15°C (14 to 5°F); full sun or partial shade; any well-drained soil; pruning not essential. Propagate by root cuttings in winter or semi-ripe cuttings in summer.

Recommended varieties
C. orbiculatus has small green flowers followed by yellow fruits that blacken and then open when ripe to reveal red seeds, rounded, mid-green leaves turning yellow in autumn.

Hedera Ivy

❝ *Ivies have never needed an introduction in the past but I think they do today. I say this because they are still dismissed as dull and boring and yet there is now a huge array of colourful varieties.* ❞

WINTER APPEAL Evergreen foliage in many shapes and shades, often variegated.
PERIOD OF WINTER INTEREST Throughout.
VALUE FOR REST OF THE YEAR Constant foliage interest for walls or ground cover.
SIZE Ranges from the small forms of *Hedera helix* often grown as houseplants, which will reach only 30cm-1m (12in-3ft) eventually, to the vigorous types like *H. colchica*, *H. h.* 'Oro di Bogliasco' and *H. hibernica*, which will reach 2 x 2m (6½ x 6½ft) after five years and as much as 8-10 x 8-10m (25-33 x 25-33ft) after 20 years.

CULTIVATION NOTES
H. helix varieties are very hardy, tolerating -20°C (-4°F); *H. colchica*, *H. hibernica* and *H. rhombea* are moderately hardy, tolerating -10 to -15°C (14 to 5°F) ; most of the other forms recommended are fairly hardy, tolerating around -5°C (23°F); types with larger and variegated leaves are generally better in full sun, but other forms tolerate light or even deep shade; may suffer leaf damage in cold winds; tolerates any soil, but is less successful in very dry conditions; pruning not necessary. Propagate by semi-ripe cuttings in summer or layers.

Hedera colchica 'Sulphur Heart'

Recommended varieties

H. azorica has matt, light green leaves. *H. canariensis* has glossy, mid-green leaves and red-purple stems; 'Gloire de Marengo', silver-variegated leaves. *H. colchica* has large, leathery, dark green leaves; among its best varieties: 'Dentata', bright green, toothed leaves and purple stems; 'Dentata Variegata', light green leaves mottled with grey-green and edged with cream-white; 'Sulphur Heart' (syn. 'Paddy's Pride'), longer, mid-green leaves tinged with cream-yellow. *H. helix* has many popular varieties including: 'Adam', small grey-green leaves variegated with cream-white, growing yellower; 'Angularis Aurea', medium, angular, glossy mid-green leaves becoming yellow tinged; 'Atropurpurea', large, dark green leaves that turn purple in cold weather; 'Buttercup', large leaves, bright yellow when grown in full sun, pale green in shade; 'Caecilia', light green leaves with frilled, cream edges; 'Cavendishii' medium, mid-green leaves edged with cream-yellow; 'Duckfoot', small, light green leaves shaped like a duck's foot; 'Erecta', an upright plant with medium, dark green leaves; 'Eva', small, grey-green leaves edged with cream-white; 'Glacier', small, grey-green leaves edged with silver-grey and cream; 'Goldchild', small, grey-green leaves edged with yellow; 'Green Ripple', large, jagged, mid-green leaves with conspicuous veins; 'Ivalace', medium, dark green leaves with curled edges; 'Kolibri', small, mid-green leaves edged with cream-white; 'Little Diamond', medium, diamond-shaped grey-green leaves edged with cream-white; 'Luzii', medium, mid-green leaves spotted with yellow-cream; 'Oro di Bogliasco' (syn. 'Goldheart'), medium, dark green leaves with bright yellow centres; 'Parsley Crested', medium, mid- to dark green leaves with curly edges; 'Saggitifolia Variegata', medium, grey-green leaves edged with cream-white and shaped like a bird's foot; and 'Très Coupé', small dark green leaves with deep lobes. *H. hibernica* has dark green leaves that are folded upwards; 'Deltoidea', small, dark green heart-shaped leaves; 'Sulphurea', mid- to grey-green leaves, edged and splashed with bright yellow. *H. nepalensis* has olive-green leaves that sometimes have toothed lobes. *H. rhombea* has unlobed, mid-green leaves.

Trachelospermum

> " *One of the climbers that makes me envious of gardeners who live in milder places, it is good at any time of year but its neat, glossy leaves have a particular attractiveness in winter when trained against old brick-work, the bronze-red flush to the foliage complementing perfectly that of the wall itself.* "

CULTIVATION NOTES

Fairly hardy, tolerating around -5°C (23 °F); full sun or partial shade, with shelter from cold winds; any fertile, well-drained soil; pruning not necessary. Propagate by semi-ripe cuttings in summer, or layers in autumn.

WINTER APPEAL Attractive evergreen foliage.
PERIOD OF WINTER INTEREST Throughout.
VALUE FOR REST OF THE YEAR Fragrant summer flowers.
SIZE 2 x 2m (6½ x 6½ft) after five years, 6-9 x 6-9m (20-30 x 20-30) after 20 years.

Trachelospermum jasminoides

Recommended varieties

Trahelospermum asiaticum has oval, glossy, dark green leaves and, in mid- to late summer, fragrant cream-white flowers that later turn yellow. *T. jasminoides* has oval, glossy, dark green leaves that turn bronze-red in winter and, in mid- to late summer, pure white flowers; 'Variegatum', leaves edged and mottled with cream-white.

INDEX

Page numbers in *italic* refer to the
illustrations.

Abies 52
Abies koreana 52, *52*
  'Silberlocke' 52
Acaena 58
Acaena microphylla 58
  'Copper Carpet' *58*
  'Kupferteppich' 58
Acaena novae-zelandiae 58
Acaena saccaticupula 'Blue Haze'
  58
Adiantum pedatum 70
Adiantum venustum 70
Adonis 58
Adonis amurensis 58, *58*
  'Flore Pleno' 58
Adonis vernalis 58
Agapanthus 76
  'Headbourne Hybrids' 76, *76*
Agapanthus africanus 76
Agapanthus campanulatus 76
air frost 7
Ajuga 58-9
Ajuga pyramidalis 'Metallica Crispa'
  59
Ajuga reptans
  'Atropurpurea' 59
  'Braunherz' 59
  'Burgundy Glow' 59, *59*
  'Catlin's Giant' 59
  'Multicolor' 59
Amaryllis 76-7
Amaryllis belladonna 77, *77*
Amelanchier 48
Amelanchier canadensis 48
Amelanchier lamarckii 48, *48*
Anemone 77
Anemone appennina 77
Anemone blanda 77, *77*
  'Ingramii' 77
  'White Splendour' 77
Anemone x hybrida 77
  'Geante des Blanches' 77
  'Honorine Jobert' 77
Anemone ranunculoides 77
Artemisia 59
Artemisia aborescens 59
Artemisia abrotanum 59
Artemisia absinthium 'Lambrook
  Silver' 59
Artemisia caucasica 59
Artemisia ludoviciana 59
  'Powis Castle' 59
  'Valerie Finnis' 59
Artemisia schmidtiana 59
  'Nana' 59
Asplenium 70
  'Cristatum' 70
  'Kaye's Lacerated' 70
  'Undulatum' 70
Asplenium scolopendrium 70
Asplenium trichomanes 70
Aucuba 14
Aucuba japonica 14
  'Crotonifolia' 14, *14*
  'Picturata' 14
  'Rozannie' 14
  'Salicifolia' 14
  'Variegata' 14
Aucuba japonica longifolia 14

Berberis 14-15
Berberis aggregata 15

Berberis x bristolensis 15
Berberis buxifolia 'Pygmaea' 15
Berberis calliantha 15
Berberis x carminea 'Pirate King' 15
Berberis darwinii 15
Berberis dictyophylla 15
Berberis x ottawensis
  'Silver Mile' 15
  'Superba' 15
Berberis x stenophylla 15
  'Corallina Compacta' 15
Berberis thunbergii atropurpurea 15,
  15
  'Bagatelle' 15
  'Dart's Red Lady' 15
  'Helmond Pillar' 15
  'Red Chief' 15
Bergenia 60
  'Abendglut' *60*
  'Bressingham Ruby' 60
  'Sunningdale' 60
  'Wintermärchen' 60
Bergenia cordifolia 'Purpurea' 60
Bergenia purpurascens 60
Bergenia x schmidtii 60
Betula 48-9
Betula albosinensis 49
Betula ermanii 49
Betula utilis 49
Betula utilis jacquemontii 49, *49*
  'Jermyns' 49
birch, see *Betula*
bittersweet, see *Celastrus*
Blechnum 70-71
Blechnum penna-marina 70-71
Blechnum spicant 70-71
Blechnum tabulare 70-71
bog myrtle, see *Myrica*
box, see *Buxus*
bramble, see *Rubus*
buds 4
Butcher's broom, see *Ruscus*
Buxus 16
Buxus microphylla 16
  'Compacta' 16
Buxus sempervirens 9, 16, *16*
  'Argenteovariegata' 16
  'Aureovariegata' 16
  'Elegantissima' 16
  'Latifolia Macrophylla' 16
  'Suffruticosa' 16

Calamagrostis 72
Calamagrostis acutiflora
  'Karl Foerster' 72
  'Overdam' 72
California lilac, see *Ceanothus*
Callicarpa 16
Callicarpa bodinieri giraldii 16
  'Profusion' 17
Calluna vulgaris 17
  'Blazeaway' 17
  'Boskoop' 17
  'Cuprea' 17, *17*
  'Gold Haze' 17
  'Golden Carpet' 17
  'Golden Feather' 17
  'Mrs Pat' 17
  'Multicolor' 17
  'Orange Queen' 17
  'Robert Chapman' 17
  'Sir John Charrington' 17
  'Sunset' 17
  'Wickwar Flame' 17
Camellia 18

'Adolphe Audusson' 18
'Akashigata' 18
'Anticipation' 18
'Berenice Boddy' 18
'Bow Bells' 18
'Donation' 18, *18*
'Gloire de Nantes' 18
'Inspiration' 18
'Leonard Messel' 18
'Saint Ewe' 18
Carex 74
Carex firma 'Variegata' 74
Carex flagellifera 74
Carex hachijoensis 'Evergold' 74, *74*
Carex morrowii 'Fisher's Form' 74
Carex pendula 74
Carex siderosticha 'Variegata' 74
Caryopteris 18-19
Caryopteris x clandonensis 18, *19*
  'Heavenly Blue' 19
Caryopteris incana 19
Ceanothus 19
  'Autumnal Blue' 19, *19*
  'Burkwoodii' 19
  'T. Johnson' 19
Ceanothus x delileanus
  'Gloire de Versailles' 19
  'Henri Desfossé' 19
  'Topaze' 19
cedar, see *Cedrus*
Cedrus 52-3
Cedrus brevifolia 53
Cedrus libani atlantica
  'Glauca' 53
  'Glauca Pendula' 53, *53*
Celastrus 92
Celastrus orbiculatus 92, *92*
Chamaecyparis 54
Chamaecyparis lawsoniana 54, *54*
  'Erecta Viridis' 54
  'Fletcheri' 54
  'Green Pillar' 54
  'Kilmacurragh' 54
  'Lutea' 54
  'Pembury Blue' 54
  'Pottenii' 54
  'Stewartii' 54
  'Wisselii' 54
Chamaecyparis nootkatensis
  'Pendula' 54
Chamaecyparis obtusa 'Crippsii' 54
Chamaecyparis thyoides 54
Cheiranthus cheiri 85
Chimonanthus 20
Chimonanthus praecox 20, *20*
  'Grandiflorus' 20
  'Luteus' 20
Chinese lantern, see *Physalis*
Chionodoxa 78
Chionodoxa luciliae 78, *78*
Choisya 20-21
Choisya ternata 20-21
  'Sundance' 20-21
Christmas box, see *Sarcococca*
Clematis 90
Clematis aethusifolia 90
Clematis akebioides 90
Clematis armandi 90
Clematis flammula 90
Clematis orientalis 90
  'Bill Mackenzie' *4*, 90
Clematis potaninii 90
Clematis rehderiana 90
Clematis tangutica 90
Clematis texensis 90

Clematis tibetana 90
Clematis viorna 90
Clematis vitalba 90
coral flower, see *Heuchera*
Cornus 21
Cornus alba 21
  'Elegantissima' 21
  'Kesselringii' 21
  'Sibirica' 21
  'Sibirica Variegata' 21
Cornus canadensis 21
Cornus mas 21
Cornus officinalis 21
Cornus sanguinea 21
  'Midwinter Fire' 21
  'Winter Beauty' 21, *21*
Cornus stolonifera 21
  'Flaviramea' 21
  'Kelseyi' 21
Cortaderia 74-5
Cortaderia selloana
  'Aureolineata' 75
  'Pumila' 74-5
  'Sunningdale Silver' 74, *75*
Cortaderia richardii 75
Cortaderia 22
Cortaderia pauciflora 22
Corylus 22
Corylus avellana 22
  'Aurea' 22
  'Contorta' 22, *22*
Corylus colurna 22
Corylus maxima 22
  'Purpurea' 22
Cotoneaster 23
Cotoneaster adpressus 23
Cotoneaster congestus 23
Cotoneaster conspicuus 'Decorus'
  23
Cotoneaster dammeri 23
Cotoneaster divaricatus 23
Cotoneaster franchetii 23
Cotoneaster frigidus 'Cornubia' 23,
  23
Cotoneaster horizontalis 23, *23*
Cotoneaster lacteus 23
Cotoneaster salicifolius
  'Pendulus' 23
  'Rothschildianus' 23
Cotoneaster suecicus 'Coral Beauty'
  23
Cotoneaster x watereri 'John
  Waterer' 23
cotton lavender, see *Santolina*
crab apple, see *Malus*
Crocus 78
Crocus ancyrensis 78
Crocus banaticus 78
Crocus etruscus 'Zwanenburg' 78
Crocus imperati 'De Jager' 78
Crocus korolkowii 78
Crocus kotschyanus 78
Crocus laevigatus 'Fontenayi' 78
Crocus longiflorus 78
Crocus medius 78
Crocus ochroleucus 78
Crocus sativus 78
Crocus sieberi
  'Albus' 78
  'Hubert Edelsten' 78
Crocus speciosus 78
  'Albus' 78
Crocus sublimis 'Tricolor' 78
Crocus tommasinianus 13, 78, *79*
  'Whitewell Purple' 78

Crocus tournefortii 78
x Cupressocyparis 55
x Cupressocyparis leylandii 55
  'Robinson's Gold' 55
Cupressus 55
Cupressus arizonica 'Pyramidalis'
  55
Cupressus macrocarpa 'Gold Crest'
  55, *55*
Cupressus torulosa 'Cashmeriana'
  55
Cyclamen 79
Cyclamen album 79
Cyclamen cilicium 79
Cyclamen coum 79, *79*
Cyclamen hederifolium 79
Cyclamen libanoticum 79
Cyclamen mirabile 79
Cyclamen pseudoibericum 79

Daboecia 24
Daboecia cantabrica 24, *24*
Daphne 24-5
Daphne alba 24
  'Bowles' Variety' 24
Daphne bholua 24, *24*
  'Gurkha' 24
  'Jacqueline Postill' 24
Daphne laureola 24
Daphne mezereum 24
Daphne odora 24
  'Aureomarginata' 24
Deschampia 72
Deschampia cespitosa
  'Bronzschleier' 72
  'Golden Veil' 72
  'Goldschleier' 72
  'Goldtau' 72
Deschampia flexnosa 'Tatra Gold'
  72
Dianthus 86
Dianthus alpinus 86
  'Joan's Blood' 86
Dianthus myrtinervius 86
Dianthus petraeus 86
Dianthus subacaulis 86
disease control 13
dog's tooth violet, see *Erythronium*
dogwood, see *Cornus*

Elaegnus 25
Elaegnus x ebbingei 25
  'Gilt Edge' 25
  'Limelight' 25
Elaegnus pungens 25
  'Frederici' 25
  'Maculata' 5, *5*, 25, *25*
elephant's ears, see *Bergenai*
Epimedium 60-61
Epimedium peralderianum 61
Epimedium pinnatum 61
Epimedium pinnatum colchicum 61
Epimedium rubrum 61
Eranthis 80
Eranthis hyemalis 6, 80, *80*
Eranthis tubergenii 'Guinea Gold' 80
Erica 26-7
Erica carnea 27
  'Adrienne Duncan' 27
  'Ann Sparkes' 27
  'Foxhollow' 27
  'Loughrigg' 27
  'Myretoun Ruby' 27
  'Pink Spangles' 27
  'Praecox Rubra' 27

'Red Rover' 26
'Springwood White' 27
'Startler' 17
'Vivellii' 27
'Westwood Yellow' 27
Erica ciliaris 27
Erica cinera 27
Erica x darleyensis
'Arthur Johnson' 27
'Darley Dale' 27
'Furzey' 27
'Ghost Hills' 27
'Jack H. Brummage' 27
'White Perfection' 27, 27
Erica erigena 26
'Golden Lady' 27
'Irish Dusk' 27
'W.T. Rackliff' 27
Erica tetralix 27
Erica vagans 27
'Mrs D.F. Maxwell' 26
Erica x veitchil 'Gold Tips' 27
Erythronium 80-81
'Pagoda' 81
Erythronium californicum 'White Beauty' 81
Erythronium dens-canis 80, 81
Erythronium tuolumnense 81
Escallonia 28
Escallonia macrantha 28
Euonymus 28-9
Euonymus europaeus 28
Euonymus fortunei 28-9
'Emerald Gaiety' 29
'Emerald 'n' Gold' 29
'Golden Prince' 29
'Kewensis' 29
'Silver Queen' 29
'Sunspot' 29
Euonymus japonicus 28-9
'Microphyllus Albovariegatus' 29
'Ovatus Aureus' 29
Euphorbia 61
Euphorbia amygdaloides
'Purpurea' 61
'Robbiae' 61, 61
false cedar, see Thuja
false cypress, see Chamaecyparis
fescue, see Festuca
Festuca 73
Festuca amethystina 73
Festuca glauca 73
'Blaufuchs' 73
'Blauglut' 73
Festuca valesiaca 73
'Silbersee' 73
firethorn, see Pyracantha
flowering cherry, see Prunus
Forsythia 29
'Beatrix Farrand' 29
Forsythia giraldiana 29
Forsythia x intermedia
'Lynwood' 29
'Spectabilis' 29, 29
Forsythia suspensa 29
Forsythia viridissima 'Bronxensis' 29

Galanthus 81
'Atkinsii' 81
'Flore Pleno' 81
'Lady Beatrix Stanley' 81
'Lady Elphinstone' 81
'Magnet' 81
'Pusey Green Tip' 81

'S. Arnott' 81
'Viridapicus' 81
Galanthus allenii 81
Galanthus byzantinus 81
Galanthus caucasicus 81
Galanthus elwesii 81
Galanthus ikariae ikariae 81
Galanthus nivalis 6, 81, 81
Galanthus plicatus 81
Garrya 30
Garrya elliptica 30
'James Roof' 30, 30
Gaultheria 30-31
Gaultheria mucronata
'Bell's Seedling' 31
'Crimsonia' 31
'Mulberry Wine' 31
'Pink Pearl' 31
'Signaal' 31
'Wintertime' 31
Gaultheria procumbens 31
Gaultheria tasmanica 31
Gaultheria x wisleyensis 'Wisley Pearl' 31
Glory of the snow, see Chionodoxa
gorse, see Ulex

hair grass, see Deschampsia, Stipa
hard fern, see Blechnum
hazel, see Corylus
heather, see Calluna vulgaris, Erica
Hebe 31
'Amy' 31
Hebe x andersonii 'Variegata' 31
Hebe armstrongii 31
'Autumn Glory' 31
Hebe cupressoides 31
'Boughton Dome' 31
Hebe x franciscana
'Great Orme' 31
'Loganioides' 31
'Variegata' 31
Hebe ochracea 'James Stirling' 31, 31
Hebe pinguifolia 'Pagei' 31
Hebe rakaiensis 31
Hebe salicifolia 31
Hedera 92-3
Hedera azorica 93
Hedera canariensis 93
'Gloire de Marengo' 93
Hedera colchica 92, 93
'Dentata' 93
'Dentata Variegata' 93
'Sulphur Heart' 92, 93
Hedera helix 92, 93
'Adam' 93
'Angularis Aurea' 93
'Atropurpurea' 93
'Buttercup' 93
'Caecilia' 93
'Cavendishii' 93
'Duckfoot' 93
'Erecta' 93
'Eva' 93
'Glacier' 93
'Goldchild' 93
'Green Ripple' 93
'Ivalace' 93
'Kolibri' 93
'Little Diamond' 93
'Luzii' 93
'Oro di Bogliasco' 92, 93
'Parsley Crested' 93
'Saggitfolia Variegata' 93

'Très Coupé' 93
Hedera hibernica 92, 93
'Deltoidea' 93
'Sulphurea' 93
Hedera nepalensis 93
Hedera rhombea 92, 93
hellebore, see Helleborus
Helleborus 62
Helleborus argutifolius 62
Helleborus atrorubens 62
Helleborus foetidus 62
'Wester Fisk' 62
Helleborus lividus 62
Helleborus niger 62
'Potter's Wheel' 62, 62
Helleborus x nigercors 62
Helleborus orientalis 62
Helleborus purpurascens 62
Helleborus x sternii 62
Helleborus torquatus 62
Helleborus viridus 62
Hepatica 63
Hepatica acutiloba 63
Hepatica x media 'Ballardii' 63
Hepatica nobilis 63, 63
Hepatica transsilvanica 63
Heuchera 63
'Palace Purple' 63
'Pewter Moon' 63
'Snowstorm' 63, 63
Hepatica sanguinea 63
holly, see Ilex
honeysuckle, see Lonicera
houseleek, see Sempervivum
Hydrangea 91
Hydrangea petiolaris 91, 91
Hydrangea serratifolia 91

Ilex 50
Ilex x altaclarensis
'Begica Aurea' 50
'Golden King' 50
'Lawsoniana' 50
Ilex aquifolium
'Argentea Marginata' 50
'Bacciflava' 50, 50
'Ferox Argentea' 50
'Golden Milkboy' 50
'Golden Queen' 50
'Handsworth New Silver' 50
'Madame Briot' 50
'Silver Milkmaid' 50
'Silver Queen' 50
Ipheion 82
Ipheion uniflorum 82, 82
'Froyle Mill' 82
'Wisley Blue' 82
Iris 82
Iris unguicularis 82
'Mary Barnard' 82, 82
Irish heath, see Daboecia
ivy, see Hedera

jasmine, see Jasminum
Jasminum 32
Jasminum nudiflorum 32, 32
'Aureum' 32
juniper, see Juniperus
Juniperus 53
Juniperus chinensis 'Aurea' 53
Juniperus recurva 'Coxii' 53
Juniperus squamata
'Holger' 53, 53
'Meyeri' 53

Laurus 32-3
Laurus nobilis 33, 33
leaves 4
Leucojum 82-3
Leucojum vernum 83, 83
Ligustrum 33
Ligustrum japonicum
'Rotundifolium' 33
Ligustrum lucidum 'Excelsum Superbum' 33
Ligustrum ovalifolium 33
'Aureum' 9, 33, 33
Liriope 64
Liriope exiliflora 'Ariaka-janshige' 64
Liriope muscari 64, 64
'John Burch' 64
Lonicera 34, 90-91
Lonicera alseuosmoides 91
Lonicera fragrantissima 34, 91
Lonicera henryii 91
Lonicera implexa 91
Lonicera japonica
'Aureoreticulata' 91
'Halliana' 91
Lonicera x purpusii 34
Lonicera splendida 91
lungwort, see Pulmonaria
Luzula 73
Luzula sylvatica
'Aurea' 73
'Marginata' 73

Magnolia grandiflora 50
'Exmouth' 50
'Goliath' 50
Mahonia 34-5
Mahonia aquifolium 34
'Apollo' 35
Mahonia japonica 34, 35
'Bealei' 35
Mahonia lomariifolia 34, 35
Mahonia x media 34
'Buckland' 35
'Charity' 35, 35
'Lionel Fortescue' 35
'Winter Sun' 35
Mahonia x wagneri 'Undulata' 35
Maidenhair fern, see Adiantum
Malus 51
'Golden Hornet' 51, 51
Mexican orange blossom, see Choisya
Miscanthus 75
Miscanthus floridulus 75
Miscanthus sacchariflorus 75
Miscanthus sinensis 75, 75
'Gracillimus' 75
'Silberfeder' 75
'Zebrinus' 75
Myrica 35
Myrica gale 35, 35

Narcissus 83
'Cragford' 83
'Dave Wings' 83
'February Gold' 83, 83
'Grand Soleil d'Or' 83
'Little Gem' 83
'Tête-à-Tête' 83
Narcissus asturiensis 83
Narcissus bulbocodium 83
Narcissus cyclamineus 83
Narcissus minor 83
Narcissus obvallaris 83

Narcissus x odorus 83
Narcissus pseudonarcissus 83
Narcissus romieuxii 83
Narcissus tazetta 83
New Zealand flax, see Phormium

Ophiopogon 64-5
Ophiopogon jaburan 64-5
'Vittatus' 65
Ophiopogon planiscapus 64
'Nigrescens' 64, 65
Osmanthus 36
Osmanthus armatus 36
Osmanthus x burkwoodii 36
Osmanthus fragrans 36
Osmanthus heterophyllus
'Aureomarginatus' 36
'Variegatus' 36, 36
Osmanthus yunnanensis 36

Pachysandra 65
Pachysandra terminalis
'Green Carpet' 65
'Variegata' 65, 65
pampas grass, see Cortaderia
pansy, see Viola
Petasites 66
Petasites fragrans 66, 66
Phormium 66-7
'Sundowner' 67
'Yellow Wave' 67
Phormium cookianum hookeri
'Cream Delight' 67
'Maori' 67
'Tricolor' 67
Phormium tenax 66
'Purpureum' 67
Photinia 36-7
Photinia davidiana 37
'Palette' 37
Photinia x fraseri 'Red Robin' 37, 37
Photinia glabra 37
'Redstart' 37
Photinia undulata 'Fructo Luteo' 37
Physalis 67
Physalis alkekengi franchetii 67, 67
Picea 56
Picea abies 56
Picea breweriana 56
Picea omorika 56, 56
Picea orientalis 'Aurea' 56
Pieris 37
'Flaming Silver' 4, 37
Pieris floribunda 37
'Forest Flame' 37
Pieris japonica 37
'Blush' 37
'Debutante' 37
'Firecrest' 37
'Grayswood' 37
'Little Heath' 73
'Little Heath Green' 73
'Mountain Fire' 73
'Pink Delight' 73
'Purity' 73
'Valley Valentine' 73
pine, see Pinus
pink, see Dianthus
Pinus bungeana 56
Pinus jeffreyi 56
Pinus leucodermis 56
Pinus montezumae 56
Pinus sylvestris 'Aurea' 56
Pinus wallichiana 56

INDEX

planning 8-9
planting 11
Polypodium 71
Polypodium vulgare 71
  'Cornubiense' 71
Polystichum 71
Polystichum aculeatum 71
Polystichum polyblepharum 71
Polystichum setiferum 71
  'Acutilobum' 71
  'Congestum' 71
  'Divisilobum' 71
  'Divisilobum Densum' 71
  'Perserratum' 71
Polystichum tsussimense 71
primrose, see Primula
Primula 86-7
Primula allionii 87
Primula x berninae 87
Primula denticulata 87
Primula denticulata alba 86
Primula elatior 87
Primula farinosa 87
Primula frondosa 87
Primula juliae 87
Primula nana 87
Primula petiolaris 87
Primula x pruhoniciana 85
Primula x scapeosa 87
Primula sonchifolia 87
Primula vulgaris 87, 87
privet, see Ligustrum
propagation 13
pruning 12
Prunus 38, 51
  'Mount Fuji' 51
Prunus azorica 38
Prunus laurocerasus 38
  'Otto Luyken' 37
Prunus lusitanica 38
Prunus serrula 51
Prunus x subhirtella
  'Autumnalis' 51
  'Autumnalis Rosea' 12, 51, 51
Pulmonaria 68
  'Lewis Palmer' 68
  'Mawson's Blue' 68
Pulmonaria angustifolia 68
  'Munstead Blue' 68
Pulmonaria officinalis 68, 68
  'Sissinghurst White' 68

Pulmonaria rubra 68
  'David Ward' 68
Pyracantha 38-9
  'Orange Glow' 39
Pyracantha angustifolia 39
Pyracantha coccinea
  'Golden Charmer' 39
  'Lalandei' 39
  'Mohave' 39
  'Navaho' 39
  'Orange Glow' 39
  'Red Column' 39
Pyracantha rogersiana 39
  'Flava' 39
  'Soleil d'Or' 39
  'Teton' 39
  'Watereri' 39

reed grass, see Calamagrostis
Rhododendron 39
Rhododendron barbatum 39
Rhododendron cinnabarinum 39
Rhododendron dauricum 39, 39
Rhododendron fulgens 39
Rhododendron griersonianum 39
Rhododendron impeditum 39
Rhododendron lepidostylum 39
Rhododendron thomsonii 39
Rhododendron yakushimanum 39
rosemary, see Rosmarinus
Rosmarinus 40
Rosmarinus officinalis 40, 40
  'Aureus' 40
  'Miss Jessup's Upright' 40
  'Prostratus' 40
Rubus 40-41
Rubus biflorus 41
Rubus cockburnianus 41
  'Golden Vale' 41
Rubus phoenicolasius 41
Rubus thibetanus 41
Rubus tricolor 40
Ruscus 41
Ruscus aculeatus 41, 41
rush, see Luzula

Salix alba vitellina 42
  'Britzensis' 42
Salix babylonica pekinensis 'Tortusa'
  42
Salix caprea 'Kilmarnock' 42

Salix daphnoides 42
  'Aglaia' 42, 42
Salix fargesii 42
Salix hastata 'Wehrhahnii' 42
Salix helvetica 42
Salix repens 42
Salix udensis 'Sekka' 42
Santolina 42-3
Santolina chamaecyparissus 43, 43
  'Lambrook Silver' 43
Sarcococca 43
Sarcococca confusa 43
Sarcococca hookeriana digyna 43,
  43
Sarcococca humilis 43
Sarcococca ruscifolia 43
Sarcococca saligna 43
Saxifraga 88
  'Arco' 88
  'Bodensee' 88
Saxifraga x apiculata 7
Saxifraga burseriana 88
  'Edith' 88
  'Eulenspiegel' 88
Saxifraga ferdinandi-coburgi 88
Saxifraga frederici-augusti grisebachii
  88
Saxifraga x gloriana 88
  'Gregor Mendel' 88, 88
  'Iris Pritchard' 88
  'Johann Kellerer' 88
  'King Lear' 88
  'Kolbiana' 88
Saxifraga lilacina 88
Saxifraga marginata 88
  'Robin Hood' 88
  'Rosemarie' 88
Saxifraga sancta 88
Saxifraga sempervivum 88
  'Sofia' 88
Saxifraga stolitzkae 88
saxifrage, see Saxifraga
sedge, see Carex
Sedum 88-9, 88-9
  'Herbstfreude' 69, 69
Sedum kamtschaticum 'Variegatum'
  89
Sedum spathulifolium 89, 89
  'Cape Blanco' 89
Sedum spectabile 69
  'Brilliant' 69

Sedum spurium 89
Sempervivum 89
Sempervivum arachnoideum 89
Sempervivum marmoreum
  'Ornatum' 89
Sempervivum montanum 6, 89, 89
Sempervivum tectorum 89
shield fern, see Polystichum
silver fir, see Abies
Skimmia 44
Skimmia x confusa 'Kew Green' 44
Skimmia japonica 13, 44
  'Bowles Dwarf' 44
  'Bronze Knight' 44
  'Fragrans' 44
  'Nymans' 44
Skimmia reevesiana 44
  'Rubella' 44, 44
  'Wakehurst White' 44
snowdrop, see Galanthus
snowflake, see Leucojum
snowy mespilus, see Amelanchier
spotted laurel, see Aucuba
spruce, see Picea
Stephanandra 44-5
Stephanandra incisa 'Crispa' 44,
  44, 45
Stephanandra tanakae 45
Stipa 75
Stipa arundinacea 75
Stipa gigantea 75
Stipa tenuissima 75
stonecrop, see Sedum
sweet bay, see Laurus

tassel bush, see Garrya
Taxus 57
Taxus baccata
  'Dovastoniana' 57
  'Fastigiata' 57
  'Fastigiata Aurea' 57
  'Standishii' 8, 57
Thuja 57
Thuja occidentalis 'Spiralis' 57
Thuja plicata 'Zebrina' 57
Trachelospermum 93
Trachelospermum asiaticum 93
Trachelospermum jasminoides 93,
  93
  'Variegatum' 93
true cypress, see Cupressus

Ulex 45
Ulex europaeus 45
  'Flore Pleno' 45, 45
Viburnum 46-7
Viburnum bodnantense 46
  'Charles Lamont' 46
  'Dawn' 46, 46
  'Deben' 46
Viburnum x burkwoodii 46
  'Anne Russell' 46
  'Park Farm Hybrid' 46
Viburnum carlesii 46
  'Aurora' 46
Viburnum farreri 46
  'Candidissimum' 46
Viburnum japonicum 46
Viburnum opulus 46, 47
Viburnum tinus 46
  'Eve Price' 46
  'Gwenllian' 46
  'Lucidum' 46
  'Purpureum' 46
  'Variegatum' 46
Vinca 47
Vinca major 47
  'Variegata' 47
Vinca minor 47
  'Alba Variegata' 47
  'Argenteovariegata' 47, 47
  'Atropurpurea' 47
  'Gertrude Jekyll' 47
  'La Grave' 47
Viola 84-5
Viola x wittrockiana 85
  'Ultima' 85
  'Universal' 85, 85

wallflower, see Cheiranthus cheiri
willow, see Salix
wind flower, see Anemone
winter aconite, see Eranthis
winter hazel, see Corylopsis
winter sweet, see Chimonanthus

yew, see Taxus
Yucca 69
Yucca filamentosa 69
  'Bright Edge' 69
  'Variegata' 69
Yucca gloriosa 69
  'Variegata' 69, 69

PHOTOGRAPHIC ACKNOWLEDGMENTS

All photographs appearing in this book have been specially commissioned from Andrew Lawson
with the exception of the following:
Professor Stefan Buczacki Back cover, 1 top, 84, 85 top, 85 bottom, 93; Eric Crichton 54, 55 left, 69 right; Garden Picture Library/Brian Carter 86
left; John Glover 61 right; Reed International Books Ltd. /Michael Boys 48; Andrew Lawson Photography 15, 18 bottom right, 18 centre, 20 right,
33 top, 35 right, 37 bottom, 44 left, 45, 51 left, 52, 53 top, 59 top, 61 left, 63 bottom, 64, 70, 71, 73 right, 77 top, 82 left, 86 right, 87, 89 left,
92 top, 92 bottom, /Waterperry Gardens, Oxfordshire 10; Photos Horticultural 19, 38, 39 right, 55 right, 67, 68, 91 left;
Harry Smith Collection 21, 28 top, 44 right, 56.

With special thanks to the following for allowing their gardens to be photographed: Barnsley House, Gloucestershire; Chelsea Physic Garden,
London; Foxgrove Plants, Enborne, Newbury Berkshire; Gothic House, Charlbury, Oxfordshire; The Priory, Charlbury, Oxfordshire;
RHS Gardens, Rosemoor, Devon; RHS Flower Show, Vincent Square; RHS Gardens, Wisley, Surrey; Royal Botanic Gardens Kew;
Savill Gardens, Windsor, Berkshire; St John's College, Oxford; University Botanic Garden, Oxford; Wakehurst Place, West Sussex;
Dr G. Walton, Charlbury, Oxfordshire; The late Primrose Warburg, Oxford; Waterperry Gardens, Oxfordshire.